The Labyrinth

and other stories of life

Edited by
Mark Worthing, Pete Court & Claire Bell

ISBN 978-0-6450377-4-6

Compilation copyright © Mark Worthing, Pete Court and Claire Bell 2021
Copyright of individual chapters remains with the author of those chapters.

All rights reserved. Other than for the purposes and subject to the conditions prescribed under the Copyright Act, no part of this publication may be reproduced, stored in a retrieval system, or transmitted in any form or by any means, electronic, mechanical, photocopying, recording or otherwise, without the prior permission of the publisher.

Cataloguing-in-Publication entry is available from the National Library of Australia http:/catalogue.nla.gov.au/.

This edition first published in 2021

Typesetting by Ben Morton

Published in Australia by Immortalise via Ingram Spark
www.immortalise.com.au

Front cover photograph by Georgina Bliss

Back cover free graphic from canva.com

Cover design concept by Stephanie Wilson

Final cover layout Ben Morton

Sponsors

We wish to thank the following organisations for their sponsorship of the Stories of Life creative writing competition and publishing venture:

Omega Writers
sponsoring each of the 2021 Stories of Life prizes.

Immortalise
supporting the publication, sales and distribution of the 2021 anthology.

Tabor College of Higher Education
hosting the official launch of the 2021 anthology.

Thanks also to **1079 Life** for their help with promotion and support for Stories of Life.

Introduction

It is a joy and a privilege to be part of the editorial team again in the sixth year of *Stories of Life*. This year we have seen many new writers emerging as well as familiar names continuing to hone their craft as they tell of God meeting them in the course of life. Some, like the writer of the story that gives this edition its title ('The Labyrinth' by Tracey Price), take us into their contemplative practice, others into crises where they have learned to trust God more deeply or have heard God speak to them in fresh ways. There are stories of conversion, healing, comfort, and courage to manage chronic health issues. Some stories describe dramatic events like car crashes and shipwrecks, others find significance in ordinary activities like running a children's program or sitting at the beach. In each story, God is shown to be present and engaged with the writer.

    I believe in the power of personal stories. Telling our stories about spiritual experience, no matter how simple, has multiple benefits. Firstly, no one else can tell our story with the same passion or conviction as we who experienced it. There is something compelling about firsthand accounts that lends credibility and perspective that fiction writers have to work hard to achieve. Secondly, putting past events into words consolidates their meaning for the storyteller, reinforcing the significance of the events. Thirdly, story is the most effective way humans have ever found for making ideas memorable. We are, it seems, wired for story, and the evidence of it goes back to the earliest known communities. Fourthly, telling stories builds community, enabling us to not only learn from each other but to grow in understanding, thus deepening connections.

Writing faith stories well increases the impact of their message. Good writing invites readers to enter in, urging them to the end, leaving them with memorable images and a resonating wisdom. In addition to amplifying the voices of Christians through story, *Stories of Life* assists writers to write well. The *Stories of Life* team provide online resources, including examples and workshops, available through the website all year round, and in June each year there is the opportunity to receive constructive feedback on draft stories.

Stories of Life would not happen if it weren't for the efforts of a number of people and the generosity of sponsors. Our major sponsor – national Christian writers group Omega Writers – enables us to offer monetary prizes to winners of the competition. Other businesses – tertiary education provider Tabor College, radio station 1079 Life, and assisted publication service provider Immortalise – provide support of various kinds so that we can continue to offer resources and publish an annual anthology of the best of the competition's entries.

Each year our behind-the-scenes organiser, May-Kuan Lim, glues together the elements of the competition, resources, and communications with unfailing kindness and diligence. A team of editors puts together the anthology. Mark Worthing deserves a special mention for being heavily involved in the editing process every year to date.

This year's judges – highly respected authors Penny Reeve (Youth category), David Rawlings (Short category) and Valerie Volk (Open category) – have given close attention to the quality of stories presented and made the difficult decisions as to who the prize winners will be. This is done 'blind' – that is, they do not know the names of the writers whose work they read. Valerie comments that reading the stories long-listed by the editors 'has been an interesting and rewarding experience…It was heartening to read of the new life that so many writers had experienced.'

Everyone has a story to tell, and we all need the encouragement of hearing stories that draw us into hope and endurance. If you have never considered writing yours, maybe 2022 will be the year when you use the many resources available to learn to tell your story in a way that touches the hearts of readers (and 1079 Life listeners in Adelaide and online), pointing to the God whose love runs through our lives.

Thank you to the writers who submitted stories this year, for your vulnerability in sharing deeply personal experiences, and your desire to encourage others with your stories of hope found in hard places. You open our eyes to the wonders of God's creation, and show examples of kindness, trust and gratitude that enrich us all. Whether you are writing them, speaking them or giving expression to them through other media, keep on telling your stories!

Claire Bell
on behalf of the 2021 editorial team

Contents

Introduction iv

The Mount Morgan Prayer Meeting 1
    Tony Koch

Don't Flush the Toilet 3
    Gaynor Faulkner

The Labyrinth 5
    Tracey Price

Grace 8
    Nadia Konik

My Guardian Yoda 13
    Ester de Boer

My Black Dogs 17
    Lynda Wake

The Turnaround 23
    Jacqueline Waters

Lord, Help Me be a Mother 27
    Sherry Thompson

A Very Perfect Day 32
    Charles Yuen

Held in My Heart 37
    Kylie Gardiner

Am I Going to Heaven? 39
    Sarah Brown

Saved by a Rat 44
    Emily J. Maurits

The Sergeant's Boots 50
    Elaine Rendell

God Sent His Angels 52
    Aileen Huf

The View from a Sardine 57
    June Hopkins

Forgiveness is a Blossoming Flower 59
    H. S. Jones

The Gift of a Rabbit 63
   Diana Davison

The Vow 68
   Jane Schope

Café La Renaissance 73
   Bernice Shen

Lessons from Toilet Training 75
   Dienece Darling

The Courage to Go 77
   Anne-Marie Doecke

An Old Car and a Hiccough 82
   Jenny Glazebrook

Proude by Name, House-proud by Nature 88
   Ai Mee Ling

Finding God on the Streets 93
   Ruth C. Hall

The Sound of Children Playing 98
   May-Kuan Lim

Birthday Catalyst 103
   Boo Hooi Jimmy Khoo

Life is Precious 107
   Jenelle Francis

Planes, Cars and God's Intervention 110
   Ivan Francis

I Wrote a Poem about It 113
   Claire Bell

We Carry On 118
   Esther Cremona

The Wise Old Owl 122
   Val Russell

Mum, Meet My Mother 127
   Jo Wanmer

Rescued 131
   Susan Brown

A Mended Heart 137
    Jenny Woolsey

Green Velvet 142
    Joy Leabrooke

The Unexpected Calling 147
    Baxter Gierus-Heintze

Small Things 151
    Shaoey C.

The Rainbow 154
    Jo-Anne Berthelsen

Miracle Baby 159
    Maggie Nerz Iribarne

I Had Been Seen 161
    Lisa Birch

My Shadow 163
    Ruth C. Hall

My Protector 165
    Karen Curran

Just in Time 169
    Colleen Russell

Immanuel: Not Just a Christmas Story 171
    Claire Bell

Pinball 173
    Tsung Chung

Twenty 175
    Robert Riggs

An Unseen Guide 180
    Craig Chapman

The Gift 182
    Juni Desireé Hoel

My First Sprout of Faith 184
    Janice D. Green

Who Would You Choose? 186
    Jenine Altmann

Tears for a Baby 188
    Jo Wanmer

Set Free from Darkness 190
    Ket Pang

Incident at Peats Ridge 192
    Jonathan Mowen

I Dined in Style 194
    Helena Stretton

Fishing for Faith 195
    R.J. Rodda

The Mount Morgan Prayer Meeting
Tony Koch

About twenty years ago my wife Jeanne and I owned and operated a small motel and caravan park in the old gold mining town of Mount Morgan, in north Queensland.

At the time, Mount Morgan had the highest unemployment rate in the state. Many people over the years had been reduced to living on welfare payments, and in some cases, this had become intergenerational. When we arrived, this situation came as a shock. We were naïve and were not used to dealing with people in these circumstances. To make matters worse, the town was in the grip of a drought.

A group of five Christians, including me, a pastor, a lay minister, and two other lay people, decided to meet every Thursday morning and pray for the town and for an end to the drought. There had been no significant rain in the area for seven years. The 'big dam' was empty, and the Dee River and Horse Creek were both dry.

After some weeks of prayer it was decided to hold a town-wide public prayer meeting in the Town Hall. We invited a group from each congregation to come and read a passage from the Bible and then to pray for God to bring an end to the drought. I was honoured to be chosen to represent my congregation.

On the night of the prayer meeting the Town Hall was packed. It seemed that the whole town had turned out!

The next day it sprinkled a bit. The scoffers said to me, 'Is that the best you can do?'

But the sprinkles soon become heavy drops. It rained non-stop for several days and nights! The 'big dam' was overflowing and the Dee River and Horse Creek were in flood. Even part of our caravan park was under water. The rain event was so big that it made the papers and even the ABC television news. Everyone knew about our prayer meeting for rain.

We gave thanks and glory to God.

At the end of that week I drove to Rockhampton for supplies. The locals asked me to talk to those Christians in Mount Morgan and tell them to stop praying for rain. The Fitzroy was in danger of flooding as well.

Afterward, our little prayer group couldn't remember whose idea it had been to hold a town-wide prayer meeting. We agreed it must have been the Holy Spirit.

Mount Morgan was never the same again.

Don't Flush the Toilet

Gaynor Faulkner

Nobody ever questioned in hushed tones, 'Is the baby asleep?' when they visited our house all those years ago. They didn't have to because they would have heard our son screaming before they knocked on our door. It's likely that they heard him from the next block. Our beautiful son bellowed day and night until he was almost two.

I sought help from several doctors and a paediatrician, insisting our baby had a severe stomach ache. They insisted there was nothing wrong with him at all. I was an overanxious mother and I was transferring it to my baby.

One consistent rule we strictly adhered to during that time was to not flush the toilet when the baby was asleep. Ever. The duration of our baby's sleep was too precarious, too ephemeral to risk being disturbed.

My husband had been travelling to work each day and had nearly fallen asleep at the wheel a couple of times due to our disrupted household. As a result, we relocated to the town where he worked when our son was seventeen months old.

Our rented department house was comfortable but needed a few roof repairs when we moved in. All day the workmen clanged and hammered above us. I laboriously patted my son to sleep that afternoon as usual. Suddenly, I was desperate for the toilet. It meant that I'd have to painstakingly extract my son from my lap without waking him up. A delicate operation.

Eventually, I managed to transfer him to the lounge and exit, quiet as a whisper, over the wooden floorboards. I savoured the rare moment of freedom before I did the unthinkable. I flushed! I couldn't believe my stupidity. Sure enough, my toddler's blood-curdling screams immediately emanated from the lounge room. There was a thud as he leapt from the lounge followed by frantic footsteps hammering the floor.

Suddenly, a deafening crash resounded from the lounge room. My heart felt like a racing car revving in my chest. I exited the loo just as my terrified toddler flung himself into my arms. Clouds of thick white dust filled the air. With my little boy clinging to me, I sprinted into the lounge room to investigate.

Bizarrely, a spluttering workman was sprawled face down on what was left of our lounge chair. He was covered head-to-toe in white dust, timber planks and sheets of iron. The entire lounge room was strewn with debris from the roof the man had just fallen through. A bomb scene.

The lounge chair was in tatters. A scarecrow. Its wooden frame was split in two under the man – in the exact spot where my sleeping baby had his head only seconds before.

In our new town the doctor ordered tests which revealed my son had a life-threatening condition necessitating an operation. I didn't see God much in our lives during that difficult time. I was too tired. But I saw him watching over us that day. God was in control when I inadvertently flushed that toilet.

The Labyrinth
Tracey Price

[The following story is really two stories that intertwine. The first (in italics) describes some key themes that have resonated with me about the journey of life. The second story intertwines into that a description of my experience of walking the Waite Arboretum labyrinth. They can be read separately and also together as one.]

Through life's journey I find myself increasingly understanding that
The labyrinth I am walking around is essentially a set space, yet the ever gently seamless turning and twisting allows differing perspectives. One may see the same things, face the same direction several or many times over throughout the walk. And yet differences emerge every time; other things come into view.

it is not about seeing what I see as much as it is about loving and considering others. Thus, I must open my 'self' to others. This increases my vulnerability but
As the labyrinth itself is the other – it gently demands consideration of 'other', and that we lose ourselves, just a little, in that process as we submit to the urge of the other.

it is openness that allows perspective to emerge, and broader perspective encourages me that I can safely engage with
Many things in view beyond the labyrinth; trees, people, stonework, they naturally appear nearer or farther away, and at differing angles as the winding, circular path draws us on, encouraging.

acceptance of life's unknowns, celebrate differences, and so better appreciate the uniqueness of us all.

This labyrinth is created by wooden logs of varying size, shape, height, texture. Beautiful, natural unique patterns etched indelibly in each log.

Like it or not, life happens as I make choices, and choices must be varied and flexible because life is

A labyrinthine series of steps. One may step around the labyrinth on the logs – which demands different stride length and balance; sometimes stepping on each log, or leapfrogging over a log, sometimes stepping on two logs at a time, or walking in between the logs on a gravel path.

full of undulations that must be negotiated as

The labyrinth centre both draws us in and compels us away. But, once reached, the centre always invites a sojourn of some kind; invitation to stay awhile, to be centred.

to flourish in a life of passive rest and active renewal includes

Being entranced by the quiet solitude of the labyrinth, one can become inured to life beyond. When it does intrude, distant laughter and quietly spoken approach of companions gently reminds of the power of even brief margins of solitude and time enjoyed cloistered away; time to recharge, to refresh. Essential renewal needed for flourishing, resilience, empowerment in reality.

spiritual meditation and deliberate growth.

The labyrinth quietly whispers its own language; intelligible, discernible only to the language of each soul.

A human reflection, image of a creator, who speaks to me through

Circular rhythms of the labyrinth; stilling the mind, emotions, allowing space and energy to the soul – to hear, to actively listen, to be immersed in that still small voice.

the Spirit who created me for a life of purposeful joy and relationship.

I walk peacefully alone in this labyrinth, except for one other soul who joins just before I exit. A not unwelcome reminder of the purpose of life; celebration, friendship, communal understanding, and spiritual joy.

Grace
Nadia Konik

It was fashionable to seek alternative lifestyles during the seventies, however we procrastinated for years. The catalyst that sent us packing was the aggressive proselytising by radical Evangelicals who'd infiltrated our family. We were determined to escape their snares, and God chuckled.

Farming was my husband Robert's ultimate goal, so he applied for work as a water bailiff to enable him to observe diverse farming ventures. We leased out our house, quit our jobs and moved to Boort in northwestern Victoria, about 250 kilometres from Melbourne. It was our experiment to see if we could adapt to farming and country living.

The first week of our experiment was disastrous. We rented a farm manager's cottage situated on a 3000 acre wheat and sheep farm on the outskirts of Boort. As Robert went to notify the farmer of our arrival, he almost trod on a huge brown snake that slithered away across the yard. When Rob informed the farmer, Norman casually asked his son if he wanted the snake for his reptile collection. My maternal instincts went into overdrive.

We arrived at the cottage to find the moving van parked outside and the two removalists refusing to enter the house because two large wasp nests hung inside the back door and toilet. With help and smoke, the nests were removed as were several huge huntsman spiders and eventually our furniture was relocated inside. That night I barely slept and I kept checking on our children, aged seven and two. The next day our new home was made liveable and the day after, our son Gregory commenced school and Robert began his new career with a spring in his step.

I was home alone with curly top Lara who'd recently begun to display an understanding of justice. If she did anything she should not have done, be it accidental or deliberate, she would place a doll facing into a 'naughty corner' in her room. The number of dolls in corners indicated the level of infringement and I knew to look out for something. Lara would then reassure me they were sorry. It was often difficult not to smile and maintain a disapproving rise of eyebrows while I searched. Today it was spilled milk on the kitchen table.

I wiped the spill and told her to let her babies out of their corners but they should ask for help in future. It was very dark in the kitchen so I switched on the overhead electric light as a reflex action. Then I glanced out the window. It was twilight outside in the early afternoon. The sky was an ominous black with billows of red-brown. Wheat fields stretched to the horizon. There was churning movement in the fields, ripping wheat upwards into a swirling mass. Sometimes it veered into trees lining a narrow roadway and snapped branches skyward. I'd heard of willy-willy dust storms and whirlwinds but this looked much more destructive. It looked like a tornado expanding in size as it ripped up everything in its path and sounded like a freight train in a tunnel, booming louder as it approached. I watched, seeing but disbelieving. We don't have tornadoes in Victoria, do we? I stood at the window mesmerised, watching the distinctive destructive funnel spiral closer.

Lara, armed with two dolls, sat down at my feet as the tornado headed directly towards us. It was only fifty metres away when I realised the glass window might not protect us. I grabbed Lara and ran into the bathroom, slamming the door behind me. I heard loud exploding bangs and cringed. I waited in the shower, shielding and protecting Lara with my trembling body. The noise dissipated and the ferocity of the wind died down. It had passed and our dwelling remained intact. Then, with Lara secure in my arms, I ventured outside. Corrugated sheet metal was stripped off some shedding. The shelter for hand milking cows was gone, except for one post imbedded into the ground. It was only twenty metres from the house. Shredded tree foliage lay scattered about.

I was stunned. The tornado was heading directly for our house but inexplicably swerved to the right, over the gravel roadway, and then abruptly turned left to leave a trail over more wheat fields where it disappeared. It had ripped up everything in its path. The sky was still heavy with menacing black clouds and blood red dust. In the distance I could see lightning strikes and I scurried to the house as large drops of rain plopped around me.

The farmer and his wife Dorothy came to ensure we were unharmed. Both admitted to praying for our safety. That did cause me to lift a questioning eyebrow. Rushing from the school bus, Gregory declared the storm was awesome! When Robert arrived home, his first words were to ask if I wanted to return to civilisation, then let out a huge sigh of relief when I declined. He'd panicked when he saw the damage driving home. Norman lost a third of his crop that day.

Over a cup of coffee Robert dropped his bombshell. Farmers informed him Norman and family were 'born again Christians'. Neither of us wanted to be preached at again and my gallant husband was adamant, if they attempted to preach just once, we were gone. We'd move immediately!

Grace

We put up our guard but the family did not preach at us, did not try to involve us in Bible studies or church attendance except to invite Gregory to join their children for Sunday School to interact with other children his own age. No harm in that; farm life can be lonely for children.

The wheat farm also ran sheep and sheep were shorn. Shearers were brought in to work and the farm yard and shearing shed bustled with calls, whistling, and noise. To the city person, the process is alien and smelly but runs efficiently, like an industrial conveyor belt of sheep and men. We were invited to observe and noted if sheep struggled they were sometimes nipped and recognised the red stain against their white fleece. The shearers worked for two days, were fed lunch at the farmhouse and when the work was completed they disappeared for their next assignment.

I became aware of the silence and decided to visit Dorothy at the farm house. As I passed her kitchen window I saw Dorothy sitting alone, cradling her head with her hands. She looked exhausted and frail. As I entered her large kitchen I could see why. The mess was jaw dropping. Red mud clung in clumps along her white tiled floors. There were food spillages and crockery everywhere. It looked like a tornado had gone through her house and with a little rueful laugh she informed me the church youth group would arrive in half an hour. My heart swelled with empathy until she added she'd just taken a moment to pray for strength to do what must be done. Any sympathy I felt evaporated. Instead I felt anger and in that moment I knew I alone must help her. If I, in the flesh, didn't help her, no one, not even God would help her! How stupid can a person be to waste time praying with so much work to be done?

It did not occur to me that God was using me to answer Dorothy's prayers. If Dorothy would have said so I would have protested and probably stormed off in a huff. I was too angry to be rational. Haughtily, I bustled about lifting the clumps of dirt from the tiles while she stacked the dishwasher. Energised by my anger, I selected the heavier, physical work. I swept and washed the floors, cleaned the tables and benches, then rearranged the chairs in the family room for the youth group. We worked at a fast, methodical pace without a break. Then we prepared the afternoon tea of sandwiches, scones and home-baked biscuits. I learnt how to cut scone-making time by half and we placed our first batch into the oven just as the church bus pulled up at the farm house. Exuberant laughter infiltrated the kitchen and brought relieved smiles to our faces. The teenagers, Dorothy assured me, would clean up after themselves and we sat down for a well-earned cuppa.

A year later, 300 kilometres away on a dairy farm, Robert and I were 'born again' and finally recognised God's leading; past the bruising by overly enthusiastic Christians to genuine, faith-filled Christianity.

Afterwards we visited Dorothy and Norman and thanked them for their numerous prayers. We discussed the events on sheep shearing day and how privileged I felt knowing God used me to answer Dorothy's prayer and I wondered what might have happened during the tornado had Dorothy and Norman not prayed. Not once did they preach at us, yet their genuine prayers and Christian lifestyle testified of Christ louder than words.

My Guardian Yoda
Ester de Boer

When I was a child, the little girl across the street from me had a box of treasures: various trinkets and costumes, a full-sized Wendy Walker doll, princess tiaras and, treasure above treasures, two real lace veils, worn by actual, grown-up brides. She never let me wear them. I was allowed to just look and touch, in wide-eyed reverence, before they were jerked from my grasp to crown far more worthy five-year old heads in our little clique.

To little girls, it's not to do with marriage, it's not about 'Prince Charming' (there Disney totally misses the mark!). It's about the sparkly, white, ever-after dress, the procession of bridesmaids behind you, the chance to be 'princess for a day'.

Fast-track fifteen years, and it's all suddenly very real. I'm surrounded by princess-perfects – other young women my age, still with baby dimples, donning lovely gowns, crowned with tiaras and lace veils, crowned with admiration… and they're so *sure*. They're so happy.

So how come I'm not?

I twist and turn the dainty ring on my finger and my face betrays my uncertainty. He reads my mind and corners my thoughts. 'It's you, you know. You're a damaged person – you're subconsciously destroying your own happiness.' He puts his arms around me, and whispers, 'I love you.' Then, 'Not many men would have you, you know, but I'm able to look past all that.'

And my head is in confusion, because I *must* be wrong. His words aren't just his – they confirm everything I've ever believed about myself. I'm at fault. I damage every opportunity to be happy.

I sabotage his love, like every other man's, turning it to anger, fists, shame…

What's wrong with me? I'm a bride – I should be happy.

I stand on the footpath and watch him drive away. He is straight-bodied and sure, righteous in his conviction. I am slumped and defeated, a miserable bride-to-be, crowned in confusion, veiled in shame.

We planned to meet later for dinner and I have hours to kill, so I wander through the trendy coffee shops and Bohemian markets, and then into Chinatown, looking without actually seeing anything, the same thought running over and over, pressing on my mind.

Looking back, I can see now that it was weird. It's a small store in Chinatown with a raised mezzanine level, the size of an average bathroom, which serves as both a staff lunch area and, I suppose, a lookout for shoplifters. The shop is staffed by a couple of young Vietnamese women who, despite the lack of customers, constantly trot up and down the stairs to the staff area to sort out boxes of goods, chatter away and answer phone calls. And there, sitting alone at a coffee table at the top of the stairs is, well… Yoda.

Okay, he isn't green, in a Jedi robe or with pointy ears. But when he catches my attention, leaning down toward me, beckoning with his withered old hands, that's the first thing that enters my mind. He looks ancient, a tiny shrivelled man with a perfectly round head and huge, steady eyes. Curious, I ascend the staircase and seat myself on the stool across from him. He smiles, pours me a tiny cup of green tea, and we sit for a while in silence, just sipping the tea, until the silence becomes uncomfortable. Then he speaks.

'Tell me about yourself.'

I smile politely and tell him what I should – my name, where I work and 'Oh, I'm getting married.' I hold up my hand to show the ring.

'Dump him.'

I'm stunned. 'Sorry?'

'Dump him.'

I can only stare. I have told this man nothing about my fiancé. How can he, a stranger, come to this conclusion? The old man leans in toward me, his eyes so calm, so full of wisdom. He speaks slowly. 'I was sent to you today to give you a message, and this is it. This man does not love you. He will not make you happy. He will abuse you and wear you down and destroy you. You must break it off today. That is all.' He leans back against the wall, then concludes, 'You may go now.'

The veil has been lifted and I find myself blinking in plain daylight. I leave.

I choose a public place – the parkland above the city. He begs with me, argues, then screams, fist raised at my face: 'I love you!' And I free my finger from its delicate gold cage and feel the weight lift from me.

It's a fortnight later when I return to the tiny Chinatown store. The two young women are still flitting up and down the stairs as though no time has passed and the two chairs at the top are empty. I want to tell him that I did it – tell him how brave I feel, how light, how happy.

'Who?' they ask.

'The old man – your granddad or something? We were sitting up in the staff area, just up there.' I point.

'Our family are all overseas, and customers are not allowed up there. It's staff only.'

'But you were there too. He gave me a cup of tea – you must have known him.'

'We would not have let you in the staff area. It's out of bounds!' She looks irritated. 'And we are the only ones who've been working here for months.'

'No,' I try to explain, 'you were both up there, and you didn't say anything. I was…'

'Look…' they have their *no time to deal with lunatics* faces on… 'this is a really small shop. I think we would have seen you.'

Then it hits me.

Yeah, they should have seen me. They had walked all around us, looked right through us…

I'm staring at them stupidly as they say, with a hint of dismissal, 'So, sorry, can't help you today.'

I step out onto the city streets, trembling, light-headed in wonder, trying to process the impossible.

And I am happy.

My Black Dogs
Lynda Wake

Recently we were gifted with a small black puppy. Right now, he is a cute ball of fluff with a bouncy spring in his step and a truck load of attitude. Occasionally in his enthusiasm to show affection, he nips and scratches us or our unsuspecting visitors. Mostly we laugh it off. Eventually, he will grow into a big black dog and, if left unchecked, these antics will injure.

My husband and children are natural dog lovers. As for me… well let's just say I need time to warm up before I open my heart to any animal invasion. Our last family pet was easy to love. A fully-trained gorgeous golden retriever, beautiful Chala became part of the family immediately following the tragic loss of our teenage daughter. Chala was a faithful friend who can never be replaced in our affections. But several months after her untimely departure, we began to ache for a new canine companion to cheer our home.

So, throughout the COVID pandemic of 2020, we searched the internet for possibilities, and asked every dog-person we knew for any dog-breeding leads. While we were waiting, we were bitten with a bad case of 'dog envy' every time we spotted a family proudly walking their very own pooch in lockdown. Meanwhile, our jaws dropped to our knees as we watched the price of puppies skyrocket beyond our means. But just when it seemed impossible, the loveable Lakeboy arrived on our doorstep with an adorable puppy-pounce. He was not what I was expecting. Not what I would have chosen. But he is a gift I am coming to appreciate – especially as I gaze into his droopy little face, filled with chocolate-brown eyes that are starting to melt my heart.

I also have been gifted with another black dog. I was not expecting this black dog either, and again, it was not one I would have chosen for myself. Nevertheless, it is mine. This one is invisible to the naked eye, but like Lakeboy, evidence of its presence runs messily through the rainy days of my grief, dragging wet grassy mud all over my life.

'Black dog has been used as a metaphor for depression from classical mythology through medieval folklore to Churchill. It acts as a symbol to externalise moods and thoughts that are difficult to communicate' (Marjorie Wallace, founder of UK mental health charity SANE).

I agree with Wallace when she says: 'It is easier to say you are having a 'black dog day' than it is to say you are depressed.' Wallace and others in the mental health profession encourage and teach people how to live alongside their black dog. Just like my visible black dog, my other black dog needs to be understood, embraced, 'taught new tricks' and ultimately brought to heel. I understand there are differing severities of depression, and while mine is not the serious clinical kind, my black dog sure bites down hard, making its mark on my life. A black beast that mercilessly rides on the tail of ongoing bereavement, this black dog visits, rather than stays. When I sense it prowling, I try to shoo it away, but its arrival and length of stay is as unpredictable as the weather in my hometown.

Both my black dogs pounce when I least expect. Lakeboy is being trained to 'stay off', but the other one pins me down for days, or even weeks before I am finally free from its clutches. It often attacks my most vulnerable places, during seasons where anniversaries and birthdays shout out my loss. This black dog knows the best moments to cause the most damage – such as unguarded glimpses of my other children struggling through the aftermath of their sister's cancer journey. Ouch. The most underhanded mischief takes place when I witness our late daughter's friends enjoying graduations, engagements, weddings and new parenthood. Danish philosopher Soren Kierkegaard said: 'The most painful state of being is remembering the future, particularly the one you'll never have.' Double ouch.

A decade on, even after all the lessons I have learned through grief, after all the victories and joys I have experienced, my personal black dog always seems to be lurking in the background, waiting for a scrap of my soul to maul and devour. According to *Beyond Blue*, an Australian organisation supporting people through various forms of depression, 'Grief and depression are quite different…but like depression, prolonged and complicated grief can lead to feelings of intense sadness, insomnia, poor appetite and weight loss…with feelings of emptiness and despair and a difficulty feeling pleasure or joy.' (*Beyond Blue*, Grief and Depression, May 2021).

So, two black dogs now hold integral portions of my life, and I hold a responsibility for them both. Both my black dogs are fairly unique and cannot be compared. But are they a blessing or a curse? With some hard work and discipline, Lakeboy should be tameable in time. The other? I am not sure whether time will make it better or even more unruly and uncontrollable. Perhaps some hard work and discipline will tame this beast too. I hope so.

My emotional black dog sure feels like a curse. During bouts of depression, shame and condemnation bark incessantly: 'You are a Christian. You shouldn't feel this way!' Darkness grows blacker and I get disappointed in myself when I surrender to these lies. Sometimes, I feign a headache to be relieved of responsibilities during these episodes. It can be too difficult to explain, even to my nearest and dearest, what is dogging my mind.

But then I take courage. I am not alone in this place. I have stared-down this black dog many times, and it has not defeated me yet. Again I return to the Psalms and allow myself to weep along with the psalmists as they pour out their pain. Black paw prints run wild throughout their laments. I re-look at stories of inspirational people who have also felt the weight of the black dog upon their shoulders. Even the great preacher Charles Spurgeon was plagued with his own black dog, as is my own gifted pastor. Yes, these black dogs may feel like curses, but they can become blessings as they increase our faith and dependency on God. Mostly, I look to Jesus. He felt the blackest abandonment upon his cross. Yet, he cried out the strains of Psalm 22 with unmeasurable faith and worshipful hope.

I have begged God to take away my black dog. But his whispered answer remains the same: 'My grace is sufficient for you in your weakness...' While I continue to grapple with the pros and cons of owning both my black dogs, one thing I have come to accept is that without my emotional black dog, I would be more isolated in my pain. The nips and scratches in my soul made by this unseen black dog encourage me to reach out, seek help and support others. As I hang out in the dog park of life, playing and running with other friends and family who live with forms of depression, I appreciate that my own black dog has granted me a greater capacity to understand and show compassion. I've also learned some cool tricks to cope with my black dog from this community who realise we are all broken and need each other. I've become 'part of the pack'. Yes, it is messy and uncomfortable, but it is a real and helpful place to belong.

My other dog, Lakeboy, is a tri-coloured Aussie Shepherd. His predominantly black coat is contrasted with quizzical rusty coloured eyebrows, neat white socks and a pure white underside. Like him, my world is not just black but filled with an underside of vivid colour: rosy red for the passionate loves I share; petal pink for my luscious new granddaughter; burnt orange for this transition season; gorgeous greens that highlight the resurrection newness in my life.

With all this in mind, today I will face the cold winter breeze and proudly take our growing black dog for his daily training walk. In spite of his somewhat annoying puppy habits, the hard work we have already put in seems to be paying off. I am encouraged by this little guy's willingness to learn and settle down when needed. I smile, even as I don my required face mask. Living alongside Lakeboy is good for my mental health. He helps me cope with my other black dog – one who seems to come alive and thrive in periods of COVID lockdown.

My two black dogs.
Not what I wanted.
Not what I expected.
Somehow I am grateful for both.[1]

---

[1] Please note, prolonged and/or complicated grief may be diagnosed as a mental disorder. Sudden, tragic loss can also trigger a variety of unhealthy mental conditions. COVID-19 experiences and restrictions may also compound underlying mental health issues. If you, or anyone you know needs medical help or intervention, contact: https://www.beyondblue.org.au

The Turnaround
Jacqueline Waters

Joanne was born upside down. Despite the efforts of several gynaecologists to turn her, she came into the world bottom first one snowy night in the English midlands, but she was none the worse for her unconventional arrival, and at a mere six pounds, a little doll. There have been several times in her life when things needed to be turned around. Sometimes she had to cope when they weren't, but her courage and faith have been rewarded by everything turning right side up in the end.

The first child of her parents and the first grandchild on both sides of the family, she received abundant love and attention. She was a pretty, blonde child, talkative and engaging. Two and a half years later she was joined by her brother. The family lived in a new bungalow in the Herefordshire countryside, surrounded by fields of blackcurrants and hops. But in the UK the inflation rate was skyrocketing and, afraid that his teacher's salary would fail to keep up with it, her father responded to a South Australian appeal for teachers, uprooted his family and planted them in different soil on the other side of the world.

'Down under,' the family enjoyed exploring their new homeland. There were trips to flooded Lake Eyre and the Snowy Mountains, expeditions to fossick for semi-precious stones and happy days on the beach. But their new life was not without its challenges: gone were the familiar lush meadows of England, afternoon teas in quaint villages, picnics on the banks of a full flowing river and walks down winding country lanes, where no one minded if they picked the wildflowers. There were no more Sunday lunches with family, no willing baby-sitters for the occasional night out and no playmates yet for the children. Joanne's mother longed for the familiar faces of family and friends, for shared burdens over a cup of coffee, and her father struggled to fit into a different education system. Soon the marriage was under stress.

Joanne was blessed with a buoyant, chirpy personality. She would need it, as just before her twelfth birthday, her mother, seeking respite from the rocky marriage, abandoned the nest and flew off to find some personal space, leaving Joanne and her brother behind. In her teens Joanne had two part-time homes: one with her father and his new wife and the other with her mother and her mother's new partner. Somehow, she managed to succeed in her academic studies and in her social life. Maybe even now the prayers her mother had prayed while she still had faith were protecting her, despite the challenges of her home situation. Joanne went to a church youth group with a friend and responded to an invitation to believe in the Saviour, though few knew about that at the time. Years later she found the slip of paper she had filled in at the bottom of a drawer and remembered her first response to God. It was the beginning of her own faith – a faith she was going to need. A few years later a friend invited her to a Bible study, and her faith took a leap forward. She attended a weekend about missions at a local Bible college and met a young man who was a student there. They were married soon afterwards.

It was a fairy-tale wedding. Pretty as a porcelain doll in her wedding gown, she looked forward to enjoying married life and having children. They bought land in the south of the Fleurieu Peninsula and built their dream home. By now she was teaching in a local school and became the breadwinner while her husband studied for a degree in education. Seven years later, as he neared the end of his studies, she began to get excited at the possibility of motherhood and even began to prepare a room as a nursery.

Once again, her life was turned upside down when her husband, without any warning, informed her he was leaving. She was devastated. It was such a shock. David hadn't seemed the fickle type and had always appeared to be an adoring husband. She was well-known and loved in her school and church communities, and many were praying for her husband to return, but it became clear that he was in another relationship. It was time to pray another way, to ask her loving, heavenly father to show her another way forward.

It seemed though that things got worse. Her school closed down. She lost her job and had to sell her home to pay her husband a share of the divorce settlement. In a very short time, she had lost everything: her marriage, her home and her job. It seemed that God was not answering, but behind the scenes he was working on turning her life around.

Joanne did not give in to self-pity. She forgave her husband, consigned that marriage to the past and looked to God for healing and a brighter future. Some light shone into it from two teaching colleagues who had also lost their jobs and offered to pay for her ticket to accompany them to England, and Joanne obtained a teaching post in an inner-city school in the north of England and prepared for new adventures overseas.

Just before she left, another thread appeared in the tapestry of her life. Her long-time friend, Brenton, had been waiting like everyone else to see if her husband was going to return. Their mutual friends were doing their best to matchmake. It worked. He received advice from a trusted pastor that, since it was obvious that

Joanne's husband had abandoned the marriage, he was free to court her. He was a quiet, shy man, a sheep farmer in his mid-thirties. Joanne had one time tried to get him to date her best friend, but that hadn't worked. He started dating Joanne just before she left for England, but it would be a while before they would see one another again.

Back in Australia Brenton waited patiently for her return and for a year ran up his phone bills with calls to Europe. Joanne returned the next summer and they went for a swim at the beach on his farm. It's a rugged beach where the Southern Ocean often uncovers many water-worn rocks. She came out of the water first and noticed a message written in stones on the beach.

'Joanne, will you marry me?'

'Yes,' she wrote joyfully.

The wedding was a happy celebration of two people who were both well-known and loved in the rural communities of the southern Fleurieu Peninsula. They moved into a home on the farm with beautiful views of the hills and sea. A few months later Joanne saw in her mind's eye a light inside her womb. It was their first child. He was born the following June and followed fifteen months later by a second son, and seventeen months after that by a daughter. Almost twenty years later they are a close-knit family, held together by love. Joanne is fulfilled in her marriage and in her dream of motherhood, training her children to be capable and caring adults.

There were times in her life when she could have sunk into self-pity and rejection. Instead, prayer and faith kept her afloat, until finally her life was turned around.

Lord, Help Me be a Mother
Sherry Thompson

My mother would always say, 'if it be God's will' or 'in God's time' whenever there was any sadness or disappointment in my life. It was her way of saying we are not in control of our lives and that God has everything in hand. She said we should pray and thank God for providing for us and trust him. Let him know that we are okay with his plans and be patient and have faith. A scripture verse comes to mind,

'I waited patiently for the Lord, and he turned to me and heard my cry' Psalm 40:1.

Shortly after my husband, David, and I were married, we migrated to Australia from the US. In a few years we knew this is where God wanted us to be and we quickly settled in to make a life down under.

A few years later I began to suffer from many female disorders, and once again the words, 'if it be God's will' came to mind, and I was okay with his plans. I got on with my life making a home on the NSW Central Coast. In 1995 I had a hysterectomy, shattering any chance of being able to give birth. My prayers then changed to, 'Why is this happening to me?' and, 'Why won't you give me a child?' I had always wanted to have children and I vowed that this would be the question I would ask God when I faced him in heaven.

Moving on with my life, I was sure there was a reason why he did not give me a child. Everything would be revealed in time. God began revealing his plan to me when my faith was strengthened as David began his ministry serving locally at Faith Lutheran Church. Then God showed me that it was his will to close the church three years later and send us to St Marys. David would be able to continue his ministry without the move interrupting my corporate career. Neat and tidy and all planned! After all, that's what my career was as a strategic planner. I measured the highs and lows against all the risks. Everything controlled and organised! They say, 'If you want to make God laugh, tell him your plans!' Everything was about to change, and I could almost feel his smile.

Shortly after we arrived in St Marys, David was called on to visit a young parishioner in hospital who was having trouble coping with the stress and pressures of being a teenager, and now she was fighting for life!

Over the next few years we saw Dani occasionally at church with her mother. When she announced she was pregnant at age 16, we both prayed asking God to keep her and her unborn baby safe. She gave birth to a healthy baby boy and named him Orion – 'Mighty Hunter'. We shared the joy of his birth and were excited as the plans for his baptism were underway. Dani asked us to be Orion's godparents. We were honoured but surprised and encouraged her to consider asking friends her own age. Dani and her mother had thought long and hard about this. She said she trusted us and did not want to ask anyone else.

Tragically, a few weeks before the baptism, Dani's mother died unexpectedly. Dani was forced to move into a refuge that provided room and board for her and Orion. The baptism went ahead as planned and it was a beautiful day.

We kept in touch with Dani over the next few months to make sure she was coping and to let her know they both were in our prayers and that we were around if she needed anything. She was alone except for her circle of friends, most of whom had their own problems. She had no family in the area and was no longer in a relationship with Orion's father.

During this time, I had decided to retire from my corporate job in the city, unsure what would come next. I volunteered at our church kindy, helping in the office when needed, and enjoyed being with all the pre-schoolers. Little did I realise how my life was about to change!

Six months later, a counsellor from the refuge centre where Dani and Orion were staying rang us and asked us to come to a meeting that afternoon with Family and Community Services (FaCS) to discuss Orion's wellbeing. They were concerned about Orion not being properly taken care of, because his mother was having difficulties coping with all the rules imposed by the centre. Being such a young single parent, they felt she needed some help.

Orion was now seven months old, and had spent time in four separate foster homes for respite care, and FaCS was now going to intervene on Orion's behalf. As Orion's godparents, we were asked to care for Orion and keep him for a period of two to five years, until Dani could get her life back on track whilst not having to worry about Orion's safety or wellbeing.

All agreed Orion needed stability in his young life and no one wanted to move him into another foster home. We were the only 'family option' as Orion's father's family did not want the responsibility. They were giving us temporary custody of Orion until after the holidays. We would then be approved as foster parents and go to court and have orders drawn up for Orion to live with us. Dani would have weekly supervised visitation with him in our home for at least the next six months.

Trying to be in control of the situation and having all my thoughts organised, I asked when they were thinking this would all take place. It was Friday evening and we had no infant seat for the car or any other equipment necessary to take care of a seven month old baby! Yet there was no panic or hesitation from either of us in accepting this plan. We both knew the Lord was guiding us. After a prayer, we left the refuge centre with some supplies, a car seat, and Orion!

We quickly settled Orion in when we got home and I went to the store to get some things that we might need for the next day. My adrenaline was working overtime. I got into the car, bowed my head, closed my eyes and let go of the tears that had been welling up inside of me. I simply prayed *'Lord, help me be a mother.'* At that moment, a voice came back to me, *'Okay Sherry, now ask your question.'* I realised, 'If it be his will' and, 'In his time' – not mine! God was giving me a child and a chance to experience motherhood – even though I was 53 years old!

Orion has now been with us for fifteen years and as his 'mum and dad' he is part of our family. We have shared his laughter, tears, first steps, first words and all the celebrations, as well as the frustrations of a toddler, and now the experiences of a teenager. Watching him grow from a small dependent baby into a thriving, bright and independent young man who loves Jesus and knows Jesus loves him has been another 'glimpse' into God's wonderful plan for us. Most importantly we have been blessed with memories to last a lifetime. The joy I have in those moments when Orion says, 'I love you, Mum' or after we say our prayers at night, 'God bless you,' fills my heart up!

It has been a 'rollercoaster' ride from the beginning with many ups, downs and sharp turns, but I know God has been at the switch saying, 'Just hold on!' God heard my cry and fulfilled my dreams of being a mother in a very special way and I have been eternally blessed because of it. I'm not sure what God has in store for us next as we journey together through this life, but I will be patient and trust him and have faith in him. I am okay with God's plans because I know that...

'I can do all things through Christ who strengthens me.'
Philippians 4:13

A Very Perfect Day
Charles Yuen

Shao King Pui's heart raced with excitement and anxiety as their taxi pulled up at the Hong Kong Outer Island Pier where a long queue of people was already lined up at the ticketing counter for the passenger ferry to Lantau Island. Large numbers of weekend tourists to that popular local destination were expected in the cool month of May.

'Ah, Pui, don't forget to be polite to Aunty Kat and her husband,' said Mrs Shao, one of her many reminders to young Pui during the taxi ride. 'They've been very kind to take you along on their weekend holiday. Remember to take your medication and injection.'

Pui mumbled a half-hearted acknowledgment but his attention was already on the huge white double decker ferry that would be his first long distance boat ride from urban Hong Kong. It would be his first holiday without his mother – in fact, his only holiday.

'You should be prepared for the reality that this baby will not survive beyond his ninth birthday,' the medical specialist had told his stunned mother not long after Pui was born. Pui had been diagnosed with thalassemia, a chronic abnormality of red blood cells. 'He will need regular blood transfusions and medication for all his remaining life, however long that may be. He will need to live near a hospital for emergencies which could arise at any time.' That conversation, fifteen years ago, had condemned Pui to a regulated mundane life. He was able to attend school, but was physically stunted and regularly suffered fatigue. Each month he took several days off from school for the mandatory blood transfusions.

After a quick introduction to Aunty Kat and her husband, Uncle Charles, and their friends, Pui's mother finally left him in the care of the other adults. She looked forward to her few days of rest. She had two older children but loved this boy more than anything else because despite his medical condition, he never caused her any trouble. Quiet, shy and inward-looking, he was also cooperative and seemed to sense her inner sadness from a loveless marriage.

Aunty Kat had been part of a church home visitation team referred by Pui's class teacher from the same church. The Shao family had been identified as one in need of special outreach care. The husband was known to be abusive to Mrs Shao and had no interest in the youngest child, whom he regarded as a liability. The other son was doing drugs. Aunty Kat and her husband, a lawyer, offered to take him for their holiday at the law firm's beachside bungalow to give the mother some respite. The young couple had recently married. Uncle Charles worked for a large law firm and the holiday bungalow by the beach was one of their perks.

Pui loved everything that he saw, heard and tasted during the long ferry ride. The vibration of the ferry engine, the laughter of the young holiday makers playing cards in the air-conditioned upper deck, the salty seawater spraying up at the stern and the piping hot Hong Kong-style tea that contained way too much sugar and condensed milk. Every sensation was new to him. The dinner of spaghetti bolognese made by Aunty Kat was like nothing he had tasted before. The scenic car ride across the mountain road to the beach and the fresh country air had built up his appetite. That night, after a shower, he laid down between the fresh sheets of his own spacious room. The first time in his life that he had a room to himself. The next morning he woke up to the smell of fried bacon and eggs, slightly browned toast and fresh instant coffee. Uncle Charles had grown up in Australia and preferred a western-style breakfast. Pui loved it. No bland rice congee or noodle soup for him that morning!

As the ladies cleaned the dishes and planned the meals for the rest of the day, Uncle Charles suggested going fishing with Pui. They had some fishing lines on hand-held reels, and hooks as well as a jar of earth worms. There were two plastic buckets for the catch.

A small creek flowing into the beach was bringing in the morning tide, so each took up their spot in the cool water, standing bare feet.

'Be careful handling the hook,' cautioned Uncle Charles as he demonstrated how to use the lead sinks and then dig the hook into the middle of the worm. 'It will be very painful if you're careless.' He then stood a few metres away and allowed Pui to fish on his own. It was important to let the boy enjoy the learning experience. Uncle Charles had done this a few times before and had no illusions about catching even a minnow. Especially not in a creek where the water was only up to mid-calf. He had read somewhere that if one cast a line 600 times one might catch a fish.

'Look, Uncle Charles,' yelped an excited Pui. They had only been standing in the creek for five minutes. At the end of his short line a silvery red thing was flailing wildly, its wet scales glittering in the morning sunlight. Surprised, Uncle Charles identified it as a small snapper about 5cm long. Beginner's luck, thought Uncle Charles to himself as he grudgingly congratulated Pui and helped him carefully remove the fish from the hook and place it in the boy's bucket. They added some sea water to keep it alive. A few minutes later Pui yelped again and sure enough there was another silvery red fish moving at the end of his line. By now, Uncle Charles was rather disappointed that he had caught nothing himself. He was supposed to be the teacher demonstrating the skill of fishing. Perhaps his inability to hide his disappointment was noticed by young Pui who was all the more pleased to gloat over his quick success.

To Uncle Charles' growing dismay and surprise, over the next hour young Pui continued to reel in minnows, one after another, while his own hook remained untouched by the apparent schools of fish heading for the boy's line. This seemed more than beginner's luck. After all, they were only standing a few metres away from each other and using exactly the same bait. Eventually it was time to return to the bungalow for morning tea. Aunty Kat was delighted to count fifteen lively minnows swimming around inside Pui's bucket and everyone teased Uncle Charles' about his own empty bucket. Had this been a competition it would have been a hands down thrashing. Pui was proud to contribute to the unexpected dinner that night of delicious fish soup cooked with fresh tomatoes and ginger.

Over the next two days Pui was happy to walk the beach by himself looking for shells and chalky stones while the adults swam and played cards and board games well into the night and took photos and videos of each other. He was unimposing and quietly enjoyed the adult company.

Too soon it was time to go back to the city and return him to his mother who was delighted that no medical emergencies had arisen and the boy seemed to have grown not only happier but healthier and more energetic after the weekend.

Aunty Kat offered to do it again a few months later and this time to include Mrs Shao if she could convince her husband to give her some time off. Unfortunately, not long after, Mrs Shao informed the couple that Pui had suddenly had a medical episode and passed away painlessly. He was only fifteen years old. But she did mention that Pui had confided to her after the holiday that he regarded the day he caught the fifteen fishes to be the highlight of his short life.

Perhaps some kind of miracle did happen that morning when Pui effortlessly caught all those fish. At a time when his life's end was drawing near, he was afforded a chance to spend a precious day in nature and experience the generosity of a loving and compassionate God.

Held in My Heart
Kylie Gardiner

I lay back against a pillow with my top pulled up and my skirt pushed down. I hadn't felt a kick yet even though we were at nineteen weeks. I hadn't even felt a light flutter like a butterfly kiss that people talked about. Nothing. The gel was cold as he wiped it over my belly.

'Do you have a tape for me to record it?'

'No,' I said. In my excitement I'd left it at home. Annoyed at myself for an instant.

'Never mind, we'll get you a photo.' The obstetrician switched the monitor on. I looked across at my husband. His eyes were alive too. The screen in front of us filled with grainy black and white pulses. Moving and flickering. The silence held a moment. A brief anticipation. Then just as quickly it was gone. He turned the screen off and picked up my hand. Why was he holding my hand?

He said, 'It was good that you hadn't brought the tape.'

My husband and I briefly caught each other's eye. His confusion mirrored mine.

'I'm sorry but your baby isn't viable.' It took a moment to register. Viable? Cold and clinical. A word you use in a business transaction. Not the language of longing and love. Stunned, I couldn't even think of a question to ask. He turned the screen back on and pointed with his pen to show us the outline of our baby.

'All the internal organs are outside the body. Limb body wall complex, very rare.'

Less than one per cent in one hundred thousand births. Incompatible with life.

'Because of the baby's size you will have to go through a full labour.'

A full labour! I was collapsing inside. Then the gel was wiped off briskly. I hurriedly fixed myself and we were steered out the door into a waiting room bursting with pregnant women. We stood at reception. Tears flowing. No-one would look at me. They all knew it was bad.

Afterwards we sat in silence in the car. We couldn't believe it. How could we be looking forward to something so much and then have it torn away? We went to the hospital and after a labour my body wasn't prepared for, we met and said goodbye to our baby girl. Such a tiny body. A body I wasn't sure I wanted to see at first because of her abnormalities. Would that be too traumatic a memory? But we slowly unwrapped the bundle the midwife handed to us and we lovingly cradled her and the tears ran and it wasn't traumatic. So small. I will never forget you, Sophie, I whispered to her, for I have held you in the palm of my hand.

'Can a mother forget her nursing child?
Can she feel no love for the child she has borne?
But even if that were possible,
I would not forget you!
See, I have written your name on the palms of my hands.
(Isaiah 49:15-17)

Am I Going to Heaven?
Sarah Brown

'We could never get married because there are things that are important to me that aren't as important to you.'

'Like what?' I said.

We had just been groping each other in the dark. We had been going out together for about six months, and despite only being in our late teens our relationship was gaining momentum.

'The outdoors is really important to me,' Gareth said.

I offered a lame reply about how it could become important to me.

'God's important to me too.'

What? Where had this come from? Since when did he know anything about God? I was the one who went to Mass every Sunday. I could probably even recite the Nicene Creed at a pinch. I had been christened in a white frilly dress, done my First Reconciliation, we had photos from my First Holy Communion and I could still picture my Confirmation dress. It reached to my mid-calf and was made of red tartan fabric with a black, narrow velvet ribbon that was tied into a bow at the neck.

Gareth made an excuse about it getting late, so I took the hint and with as much poise as I could muster, retreated to my bedroom.

A feeling of dread pervaded my mood during the weeks that followed. It was obvious to me that my feelings for Gareth weren't reciprocated with the same intensity. It was my first experience of being in love. By July of 1990, I was yet to turn nineteen, but I had already decided I wanted to spend the rest of my life with him.

I was getting ready in Gareth's room for a Dining-In night at the RAAF base while he'd gone to have a shower. Beside his bed was a maroon-covered book with *God's Word* written in large white font. It didn't occur to me that it could be a Bible. In my experience the Bible wasn't for personal reading; it was a tome that the priest kissed at various times during Mass.

I peeked into the maroon book and was surprised to discover it was a Bible. Copious verses and paragraphs were highlighted in different fluorescent colours. He'd scribbled notes in black ink in the margins but they were too messy for me to understand. Next to the digital clock radio and sitting under his garrison cap was a thin book that reminded me of a school textbook. I sneaked a look in that too and was fascinated by the answers he'd written in response to questions like:

What impact do you think this chapter would have had on its original readers/hearers?

What do you think verses 3-10 teach us about loving our neighbour?

What steps can you take this week to put into action the truths you have learned from this text?

All over the pages was more illegible handwriting. I was intrigued by the content. I'd never met anyone that interacted at an intellectual level with the Bible the way that I observed here. I hadn't been encouraged to read it or engage with the claims it made, including the implications these might have for my life.

Gareth always had really quick showers and I didn't want him to find me snooping through his stuff so I stashed the books back, next to the clock.

During the next couple of months Gareth talked more openly about his Sunday evening commitment of Bible study followed by church. He even came to Saturday night Mass with me once. I noticed that he listened intently to everything the priest said during the homily. I zoned out.

He asked me if I was interested in meeting with Sharon, to study the Bible. She was the wife of an army officer that Gareth had been reading the Bible with for the past few months. I started to worry that this God-thing was going to be a deal-breaker in our relationship, so I agreed.

My intrigue in Gareth's faith grew steadily during the intervening weeks. Arrangements were made for me to meet Sharon in a small, white church on Swanston Street in Melbourne. As I pushed against the large wooden door it opened easily. I was fascinated by the building but also excited to meet this woman Gareth had told me about.

I cautiously entered the cold and dark hall.

'He...llo.'

'You must be Sarah,' the chic, twenty-something blonde said.

Sharon's voice purred and I immediately felt under-dressed in my not-quite-blue, not-quite-purple Kathmandu polar fleece jacket.

We entered the cosy sacristy where a small, orange heater rattled, barely lifting the winter chill from the air. I was intrigued. Why would such an immaculately presented woman want to meet me in a musty old church? This felt like a blind date.

She instantly put me at ease with her warm smiling face. I felt comfortable enough to ask her a question that had always bothered me.

'Do you think you can know if you're going to heaven?'

'I think the Bible does have something to say about that,' she said.

From a young age I'd had a strong sense that I could know whether or not I was going to heaven. I knew there was an answer but I hadn't been able to find it yet. Surely the Bible didn't have the answer to this question, did it?

Sharon welcomed a whole lot of my other questions during our first meeting together and she seemed genuinely interested in helping me to find the answers. She suggested we continue to meet at the same time each week.

Our catch-ups became the highlight of my week. In between our meetings I would devour the study material and I couldn't wait for Wednesdays to come around. I was like a sponge. Sharon always referred me to the Bible to find the answers to the questions I had about human suffering, death and the hereafter. It was so clear and straightforward. I couldn't believe I hadn't learnt these simple truths before now.

I loved the way the flimsy tissue-like paper stuck to my fingers as I thumbed through the Apostle Paul's letters to the ancient churches. Not all the epistles were immediately clear in their meaning but I discovered that if I applied myself to studying the text there were answers to be found. It was as though the words on the page were written specifically for me and I was overwhelmed with joy to discover that I could gain access to heaven through Jesus' death on the cross for me. Christianity and its teachings helped me to understand the solution for everything that had gone wrong with the world.

Am I Going to Heaven?

Sharon left my ambit almost as quickly as she had appeared. Her army officer husband was posted to Canberra and she was mostly gone from my life.

Gareth's pursuit of the outdoors continued. I learned that he had come to understand the gospel only about six months earlier. I was devastated – as well as confused – when he ended our relationship. But I sensed his convictions about living for Jesus were not as firmly as established as mine. Despite my sadness I found great comfort and assurance that God was in control of my circumstances and that he would use them for my ultimate good.

I joined the Christian Union at RMIT. I attended the prayer meetings as often as possible and actively sought out Christians studying in the same course as me. I found a church that taught the Bible and was delighted to find a large group of young people who were also followers of Jesus. Sunday nights became the new high point of my week. I was overwhelmed with the knowledge that God loved me; God knew me intimately and wanted to involve me in his plans. The open invitation to live with him forever in heaven included anyone else who wanted to take him up on his offer. This was such great news. I told everyone and anyone who was willing to listen.

Saved by a Rat
Emily J. Maurits

Lorie opened his eyes in the darkness. Because this was his house, and had been for many years, he knew how to read the blackness slung across his bedroom. It was 4 o'clock. A jolt of excitement skittered through his chest.

You've looked after me for twelve years, Jesus. Look after me today.

He sat up, turned on the light, and checked his phone just to be sure. The PMV truck would swing by at 5am, driven by a neighbour who'd promised to give him a lift. Lorie just had time to get dressed and double-check his passport was safe in—

Where was his passport?

Lorie stopped. He twisted his neck, throwing his eyes over every lamp-lit surface. Nothing. He threw himself out of his bed to the ground and tore open his suitcase. He fumbled through his clothes, fingers shaking. Nothing. He tore open his other box, sliding his hands down the sides and praying for the brush of paper. Nothing. Gumtrees and sparkling beaches, images he'd seen on the PNG TV channels rose before his eyes, taunting him.

He wiped his forehead, but didn't dare stop long enough to wipe his neck and back as well. He'd put his passport somewhere safe, but where? His brain was turning slowly – too slowly. He pictured a stern official shaking his head: No passport, no visa.

He checked the time. It was 5 o'clock. His stomach dropped. *Oh Lord, show me my passport.*

'Lorie!' He jumped and looked up, before realising the voice was coming from downstairs. He was still getting used to having his newly-widowed mother living with him. 'Lorie!' she called again, 'The truck's here!'

Lorie opened his mouth, but nothing came out. How could he say he'd lost his passport? The words were impossible to form with his dry tongue; to speak them aloud would be to admit they were true. He swallowed. 'I'm not ready!' he called. 'Tell the truck to go on without me.'

'Not ready? But Lorie–'

'I'll find another way!' Lorie sunk back against the side of the bed. He gave his suitcase a kick. The gurgle of the departing truck came through the curtained window behind him.

Lorie closed his eyes. 'Oh God,' he prayed, 'if it's your will for me to study your Word in Australia, please show me where my passport is!' And then, in the still heat of pre-dawn, he heard a noise.

12 years earlier

They were dead. Lorie knew that immediately. In the parade of waxen faces he recognised the features of people he'd once known. That man had died last year; she had died before that; that child had died last wet season...

One corpse broke away and came up to him, shambling as only a dead body can, and Lorie tried very hard to wake up.

No luck.

'Lorie,' said the dead man, and from his decaying mouth, it didn't sound like his name at all, but a curse. 'On this bed I died.' It was a statement, matter-of-fact, and Lorie knew with utter certainty that the corpse was telling the truth.

'Lorie,' said another of the dead, 'on this bed I also died.'

Then they were around him, reaching out, pressing forward: 'I died – she died – we died on this bed.' It was an inescapable pledge. *Lorie, you also will die.*

He woke up. The room was strange, his heart loud, and louder still were the voices from his dream, calling to him out of the shadows: *Lorie! Lorie–*

'Dad!' Lorie shouted, any embarrassment fleeing before his fear. *He was too young to die!*

A grunt, a shuffle by the side of his hospital bed. 'What's wrong? Are you worse?'

'I - I had a bad dream.'

'Turn around, sleep the other way.'

Despite the weakness in his legs and the burning in his stomach, Lorie managed to reposition himself. He got as comfortable as he could, then closed his eyes. *I should pray.*

All the times he'd skipped church or come late, all the times he'd gone drinking with his friends and spared no thought for God rose in front of him, like a second parade of death-bringers. *No, I can't pray,* he thought, and fell asleep wishing for a doctor and for morning.

At last the sun rose, doubling the temperature inside the tiny medical clinic and intensifying the sharp smell of disinfectant. It did nothing, however, to stop the coldness spreading through Lorie's body. The creeping chill had begun as suddenly as the burning. Lorie remembered his dream. What would happen when the chill reached his heart?

'Mum? Can you get the nurse?'

The nurse, her starched uniform glowing in the morning light, was even less reassuring than the day before. 'We don't know what's wrong. Perhaps an ulcer, perhaps something has ruptured... I'll give you another injection.' She slid the needle into Lorie's muscular bicep and, when she pulled it out, shook her head. 'That's it. There's nothing else we can do.'

Lorie, on this bed you will die.

'Mum? I want to go home.' Lorie's throat swelled. 'I don't want to die here!'

'The ambulance driver is sick,' the nurse said. 'He cannot take you home.' She left, and Lorie's mum soon followed.

She doesn't want to watch me die. Lorie lay on his bed, burning from the inside, freezing on the outside. Everything he had heard at church suddenly returned to him, everything he had treated as unimportant compared to enjoying his life as a twenty-two year old. If I die on this bed, he thought, I know where I will go, and it will be worse than this agony.

Lorie, on this bed you will die.

If only I could pray. But I never even bothered to get my own Bible, how can I pray? Lorie swallowed, his heart thudding in his ears like a count-down timer as the shadows began to lengthen and the coldness crept up his body. Praying wasn't the only thing he couldn't do. Since the pain began he'd been too weak to stand, in too much pain to eat. He saw the anxious faces of his neighbours, and remembered the tears of his siblings and the prayers of his parents.

Lorie, on this bed–

The nurses can't help me, he thought. The ambulance driver can't take me home. My parents have left me, and I can't walk. Only one person can help me.

Can I really pray? He breathed in. He had to. But what could he say? He remembered what he'd learnt as a child, and as he lay alone he whispered the words. 'Lord, I'm a sinner,' he said. 'Please forgive me. Help me.'

Present day

The rustling sound intensified. 'Amen,' said Lorie quickly. Just his luck. He'd never had a rat inside his house, and now just when he'd lost his passport and missed his lift…He moved across the room and grabbed his machete, frustration lending him strength. He would find the rat and kill it.

A rustle on the far side of the room. A flash of brown. Was that a whiskered nose peeking out from behind his suitcase? Holding his breath, Lorie inched forward. One step – two steps – a plump brown body streaked out into the open. Lorie swung as the rat hurdled in between his legs, but the animal was faster and the metal blade skidded on the timber floor. *Look at you,* Lorie's packed belongings seemed to sneer, as he and the rat went round and round. *Chasing a rat instead of going to Bible College. Where is your God now?*

Lorie could feel himself losing his grip on the machete and stopped to wipe his palms on his shorts. The rat stopped too, as if waiting. Then a dog barked outside, and, paws scrabbling on the hard floor, the rat took a flying leap towards the window. Lorie scooped up his machete and marched over to the swaying fabric.

Now he had it. He drew open the curtain as if pulling off a Band-Aid – and there was his passport, lying on one of the horizontal glass slats, exactly where he had placed it the previous night.

Lorie looked at the rat on the windowsill, poised to flee, and let his machete drop to the ground. *Lord, you sent me a rat to find my passport!* As his knees touched the floor, the precious blue book clenched in both hands, he heard a throaty roar.

'Lorie? Lorie! The truck's come back! The driver must have forgotten something.'

The rat that had been spared scuttled through the glass slats and out into the early morning. The man who had been spared all those years ago slipped his passport into his pocket, picked up his suitcase, and walked down the stairs, shouting, 'I'm ready now!'

And across the ocean, in the darkness of pre-dawn, the Australian sun began to rise. God was not finished with Lorie yet.

The Sergeant's Boots
Elaine Rendell

The vicar's sermons were always interesting, sometimes thought-provoking, and on one memorable occasion, positively life-changing. The story he told us that day may not sound significant to other people, but it affected me profoundly and completely changed the way I understand and practise my Christian faith.

The theme on that chilly Sunday morning in 2014 was 'Forgiveness'. I had always struggled with the idea of forgiving someone who had said or done something hurtful to me or a person I cared about. Why *should* I forgive him or her? They do not *deserve* to be forgiven!

As part of his sermon, the vicar told us a story about a young Christian soldier who was just beginning his basic training. As often seems to be the case, the sergeant was a demanding taskmaster, and treated the young recruits with contempt. One evening, as the recruits were preparing for bed, the young soldier knelt next to his bunk and began to pray. His kit was prepared for the following day: rifle cleaned, backpack checked, boots clean and shiny. Seeing the young man kneeling on the floor, his head bowed in prayer, the sergeant removed one of his own boots, still dirty from the day's activities, and began to hit the young man around his head and body, telling him in no uncertain terms what he thought of 'Bible-bashers' in general and praying in particular. The young man rose from the floor and got into the bunk without responding.

'That night,' the vicar continued, 'the young soldier got his revenge.'

'Here we go,' I thought. 'Meatloaf in the sergeant's boots? Surely not serious harm or murder?'

'The next morning,' the vicar told us, 'the sergeant found his own boots cleaned, polished and sitting neatly next to his bed.'

I felt like *I* had been hit over the head: the jolt was almost tangible. This was so unexpected, this act of kindness and respect as 'payback' for such poor treatment by the sergeant. I remember thinking, 'I'm *so* wrong! Everything I think is upside down and back to front!' It occurred to me that my reaction to the abuse suffered by the young soldier, and my expectation of 'revenge' in the form of retaliation, was the exact opposite of what Jesus teaches us to think and do. Thinking about the story later that day, I realised that we forgive the wrong-doer and treat them with love and kindness, not because they 'deserve' it, but because this is the love for one another that Jesus preached and modelled during his time on Earth. When Jesus told his listeners to love their enemies, this was the love he was speaking of. I resolved at that moment to change my thinking and actions, and to try to 'do' the love that Jesus teaches us.

I cannot, in all honesty, say that I am always successful in this endeavour. I am, after all, 'only human'. But the wake-up call I received that Sunday morning is never far from my consciousness, and changed my life by changing my thinking about what it means to be a Christian. I will always be grateful for that sermon, and will do my best to give full effect to its message of love.

God Sent His Angels
Aileen Huf

My husband Derryl and I farmed all our lives and looked forward to our annual fishing trip at the coast. Our first boat was a tinny. We upgraded to our pride and joy, 'Deena Sea' – an 18 foot open runabout purchased upon our retirement to Port Macquarie on the mid-north coast of NSW. We fished whenever we could and our outing on the last day in 2003 started out as usual, with Derryl, me and our friend Wayne.

We left the boat ramp at 6am and called Volunteer Marine Rescue (VMR) to report our intention to fish about twenty kilometres north of Port Macquarie at Point Plomer. We had three people on board and our Estimated Time of Return (ETR) was 2pm, or sooner if the wind came up.

We were about five kilometres offshore when we lowered our anchor in 60 metres of water with fish showing on the depth sounder. My husband Derryl had to let out extra anchor rope so the swells wouldn't lift the boat off the anchor. With the anchor holding, the water roared past and we instantly realised that the raging current was unfishable. According to the GPS, the current was 9 kph! We decided we would move into the more protected Barry's Bay.

When retrieving the anchor, the procedure is to drive the boat in a big arc, then clip a ball onto the rope to hold the anchor up while the rope is retrieved. This day, with so much rope out and with the strong current, before the rope could be retrieved it washed back under the boat and around the motor leg, stalling the motor. This in turn anchored the motor to the anchor and whipped the boat around 180 degrees. The back of the boat rapidly filled up with water from each swell and before we could untangle the motor or cut the anchor rope we were thrown out as the boat flipped!

As shock was replaced by reality, I saw that I was drifting away from the boat. I made some panicked strokes to get back to the boat. Derryl grabbed me and we were able to stand on the bow rail, but the only thing to hang on to were the little D clamps that are used to pull the boat onto to the trailer. Our friend Wayne managed to climb onto the hull. Derryl, in bare feet, found it painful to stay on the bow rail, so he moved to the back of the boat to the motor. The waves soon increased in size and kept picking him up and dumping him onto the propeller blades, or washing him off and making him swim back.

Suddenly I realised how quiet it was. As I looked at Mount Elephant, I pointed out that we were adrift and travelling fast. We estimated that we had capsized at approximately 8:15am, and knew that no one would even begin to wonder about us before our ETR time of 2pm. We took stock of our situation. The length of anchor rope that was tied to the bow rail was threaded through the D clamp, up and over the hull for Wayne to hang on to, then back to the motor for Derryl. By this time, Derryl was being washed off so often that he had tied his wrists to the rope. All I could do was pray that he had the strength to keep pulling himself back onto the boat.

The anchor on the other end of the rope was being towed along and this, it turned out, was a blessing as it stabilised the direction of the boat with the swells. We constantly prayed, 'Lord, we are totally in your care. We have absolutely nothing to offer. You have provided just enough – the floating hull, the rope and no injuries.'

By 2pm we had drifted about 35 kilometres south and were off the coast near Laurieton. The current had also taken us further away from land. We knew that the alarm should be raised when we didn't answer the radio. I was thinking, 'We'll see the rescue boat soon,' and, 'It's daylight saving time so the extra hour will give them time to find us before dark.' A few ocean liners steamed past between us and the shore but none were close. In strong currents they sail closer to land, trying to find an easier run. We prayed that none of them would run over us.

As the day began to draw to a close and we faced the prospect of spending a night in the ocean, I looked up to see an amazing cloud formation. Apart from a bank of cloud on the horizon it was the only cloud in the sky and it was in the form of a dove. Normally clouds change shape or dissipate quickly with a wind blowing, but this magnificent dove – for me, the Holy Spirit – remained for a long time with the sinking sun highlighting its head. I shared this with Wayne. Just before sunset the cloud changed into a boat with a sail! I felt privileged to have seen this sign of God's presence with us. I thanked God and begged him to send the promised boat... preferably right now!

With nothing to do but pray and think for hours, I resorted to bargaining with God. 'If you save me I will do...?' Dare I bargain with God? Abraham did in Genesis 18. 'I know I'm not Abraham,' I prayed, 'but you have told us we can come to you when we are in trouble and you hear our prayers...Well, we are certainly in HUGE trouble...please!'

And then I thought – maybe God is not going to rescue us!? I'd better prepare for that. I went through what I had learned in Confirmation and Luther's evening prayer. 'Father, into your hands I commend myself.' After that came a real peace.

More ships passed through the night. We saw some fireworks in the towns as we drifted by and our first time check came when a ship blew its horn three times…Ah, midnight! Wayne wished us a Happy New Year! For company we had a half moon until it set about 2am and then it was really dark until first light at about 4:45am. We didn't talk much, just encouraged one another.

Daylight was welcome and I was still begging God for my sailboat. The wind was strengthening, and the swells were now around two and a half metres high. I lost track of the number of times Derryl was washed off and noted with concern that it took him longer each time to get back onto the boat.

By this time we had been in the water for more than 24 hours, had drifted about 130 kilometres south, and were about 18 kilometres from land, which we could now barely see. Wayne informed us there was a ship coming our way. Soon a huge bulk carrier named *Anangel Pride* steamed past, about 150 metres away. It seemed not to notice our screams, or seen Wayne, who was madly waving a piece of red spray jacket that had come out from under the boat the previous day.

Suddenly, black smoke belched out of the chimneys and ever so slowly the ship circled us and stood by. What a sight! We now know that we were spotted by the watchman on this Greek vessel. He at first had thought we were a FAD (a Fish Attracting Device) and changed course to get a better look – and then reported our position to Sydney water police.

I thanked God for his sense of humour. A small sail boat was all I had expected, but God sent 'an angel' in the form of a 249 metre ship! And just to reinforce the point, in no time at all three helicopters arrived. The first sent down a frogman who harnessed me up and winched me into 'Angel 1'.

Two medics pulled me through the open door of the helicopter and wrapped me in blankets and took my blood pressure. 'How is it?' I asked.

'Better than mine!' replied the medic. They said that after twenty six hours in the water they were expecting to pick up bodies. Derryl and Wayne were winched into the second helicopter, aptly named 'Angel 2'.

My first drink of water never tasted so good. Hugging our family and friends never felt so good. Some things I once considered important no longer are.

Later, we were able to express to the flood of media that our rescue was totally in God's hands. The prayer support given to us by family and friends all over Australia was immeasurable and priceless. We continue to praise God for our rescue. He is not finished with us yet.

The View from a Sardine
June Hopkins

On a lazy summer's afternoon, my sister and I mapped out our futures, while lying on our backs beneath a leafy overhang from a gum tree beside our home.

'I am going to be the first female prime minister of Australia,' I proclaimed. At age eight, I was nothing if not ambitious. My younger sister was similarly inclined.

'I am going to be a famous singer on the radio,' she enthused. I thought I had a better chance at achieving my goal than she did, as I didn't think much of her singing. Still, neither of us had any idea as to how we would progress to our chosen occupations.

A mischievous crow dropped a hard piece of bark from somewhere above us, which landed with a dull thud on my face. I scrambled to a sitting position, feeling for any damage as I yelled at it. My sister inspected my cheek and advised me in solemn tones that my skin was intact.

'They wouldn't let you be prime minister if you had a scar on your face,' she informed me.

'If that is true then I will ask God to make me a mother with twelve children,' I replied. We resumed cuddling our dolls, leaving lofty ambitions to be further discussed another day.

This dialogue encapsulates a lifetime issue for me – the tension between being ambitious and being a Christ follower. Years later, when I overheard my then four years old daughter warbling 'Jesus wants me for a sardine,'* my reaction was *I think it's true, but I really wanted to be a shark.*

Ambition and drive have always featured strongly in my life, tempered by a love of relationships and family. The tug between a yearning to achieve, but an unwillingness to sacrifice too much, describes me best. As a Christian, faith has undergirded my actions in life, providing a safety net when I've met with failure, and a stabilising force when I've achieved.

I have happily experienced success in nursing, and some writing, but I discarded the notion of a political life long ago. I've also had my share of failures. I didn't have twelve children. God blessed my life with fourteen grandchildren, all of whom I love (helping me see I would never have coped with a dozen of my own).

My family is my greatest success story.

Psalm 139 is a lifelong favourite of mine. Verse twenty-one describes life as an open book, in which all the stages are spread out before God, who has prepared every day of our lives. He is the author of my life book.

Reviewing my life thus far, it is more sardine than shark-like. I am okay with that as I am God's sardine.

* The original song was 'Jesus wants me for a sunbeam'.

Forgiveness is a Blossoming Flower
H. S. Jones

They were there, on the Facebook post. I could recall seeing those eyes before. My obscuring vision compelled me to message Mother with a screenshot, questioning my memory in the hopes that I was wrong. My text was acknowledged with 'I'm coming home now, my dear' in a delayed response, raising my perplexed heartbeat as her working day was yet to finish for another two hours. What was happening? Was it me in the news article?

I felt my stomach tighten as I heard the moan of the garage door followed by Mother's hurried footsteps against the concrete tiles.

'Where's Heather?' she fretted through the house.

'I'm here, Mum' I muttered, voice breaking in a tightening throat. 'What happened?'

Mother's weak gaze meeting mine, she sat beside me and released a painful sigh. 'In 2016, you were videoed getting changed at the chiropractor.'

A nauseating feeling of harsh realisation began to engulf me. I could not bring myself to believe that the eleven year old in the news article was me. Abruptly, I felt detached from my body like it had been stolen from me. Never did I foresee becoming objectified like that. By betrayal. By abuse of authority. Eleven-year-old Heather had no control.

Mother's words of foreign truth urged a chest of distant memories in my mind to break open. My vision was taken back to that day. Back into that building. Back to his greed.

I was sitting in the waiting room beside Mother, watching the lady at the front desk organise her papers and listening to the scratch of her wiggling computer mouse. My curiosity was interrupted by his distant laugh as he farewelled a patient and approached Mother and me.

'Okay, next on my appointment list I have Heather and Esther,' he said with a welcoming smile.

Gaze recollecting still, I felt the gentle pressure of Mother's warm hand against my bare knee.

'I'm sorry, Heather. I felt terrible when I found out from the police. I just had no idea!' lamented Mother.

'You wouldn't have taken me there if you had known what he was doing.'

Lips trembling and eyes assembling a collection of tears, I walked to my room. I stood in solitude, eyes darting around my ghost-quiet room, not knowing where to go or what to do. I was aware of child pornography, yet I had never thought it would happen to me. Without me knowing.

2016. I had been eleven. I had been a child and was growing up, innocent to the world, and was taken advantage of.

I felt sick to the stomach at the thought that he believed he had it all. He had believed his bitter secret would forever be his.

The next day, Mother drove me to the local garden centre. My nose took in the luscious floral scent and my heart was in awe at the diversity of bright colours. As I moved around, my gaze was enticed by a withering plant overwhelmed by the shadows of the concrete wall. My heart sank as I read on the tag: 'This flower will bring joy to your garden'. It haunted me that such beauty could not fulfil its purpose due to its hostile environment.

As the sun plunged below the Adelaide Hills, my head coiled into a tight knot as I sat beside Mother. Car toiling upwards, I felt gravity push against my face, prompting uninvited thoughts to recollect.

'How long were you keeping it from me?' I queried.

Moving her hand down the steering wheel, Mother held a dim gaze on the road ahead. 'Two years,' she admitted.

Silence arose like a moon on a clear night and settled in reverence.

'I never wanted you to find out.'

Leaning against the car door, my eyes fixed beyond the car window and upon the collection of assembling stars ready to shine. I saw the moon. The moon. A distant moon staring down upon the world like an eye. It sees everything. It sees you. And it saw me.

Later that night, my stomach burned. It burned like a fresh fire. A brewing cauldron of many emotions. A potion of poisonous disbelief.

Arriving home, I saw a newspaper lying on the dining table calling for attention. My legs gravitated toward it like a magnet. I had no control. My arms flicked the front page. The crinkle of the coarse paper sought to affirm the truth. I saw it. The article's title spoke the age I was that day. Eleven.

'I just wanted to see more boobs,' I read.

Those eyes. They didn't see the flourishing personalities of women. The warmth. The intelligence. The kindness. The individuality. The God-given purpose each woman has in the world. Instead, that man possessed the wickedness to disregard the bright souls of women. He sought a short-term dopamine high off the private world of a growing child. Don Juan controlled his kaleidoscope mind within a perpetual spiral of destruction. Thought he had the power. Thought his secret would forever be his.

The growing potion overflowed in my stomach. It crawled up my spine and into my brain. I felt the potion begin to twist my thoughts of emerging sympathy for him into pure hatred. I needed help. Promptly, clinging onto my last fragment of logic, I emailed the school counsellor.

A wave of peace fell upon me as I knocked on the counsellor's white door. I felt that this decision would enable me to rediscover the path to healing. My aching soul was welcomed by the glisten of her sympathetic eyes and radiating smile. Through each word of pain I released, I felt the heaviness of the overflowing emotional poison within me supernaturally evaporate. The remnants of my situation began to bloom with a garden full of radiant flowers as the warm rays of the ascending sun farewelled the bitter shadow of the moon.

I am beginning to understand the meaning of forgiveness.

The Gift of a Rabbit
Diana Davison

As the aircraft touched down on warm tarmac, the sun blinked her goodbyes for the day. We were on a family holiday to Bali, Indonesia. A tropical island laid back with its alluring atmosphere. Palm trees, beaches, flying kites and the easygoing, smiling Balinese people created an enchanting paradise. With enthusiasm, we exchanged an Australian winter and woollen jumpers for lightweight clothes and sunshine. As with every planned holiday, I ensured entertainment was plentiful for my children. Coloured pencils and drawing books, stickers, reading material, puzzles, cuddly best friend toys. And, tucked inside their pull-bag, a small wrapped present to open on arrival. My husband described the effort and planning I put into the girls' being joyfully occupied as akin to a military operation. Yasmin, my eldest daughter, was an avid reader. Books were her eye candy. And always by her side, or on her lap, or in her arms nestled her constant companion and favourite friend, Gaga rabbit. My youngest daughter, Chloe, loved stickers and puzzles. Her treasured buddy was brown Penny bear who had more outfits than any doll I knew.

When the airplane landed, my two youngsters were excited to get off. Seven hours of sitting was a protracted time for a five- and seven-year-old. Prior to disembarking the aircraft, making sure nothing got left behind, I did a family body and bag count. Husband and bag, check. Eldest daughter with Gaga rabbit and bag, check. Youngest daughter with Penny bear and bag, check. All was good. With belongings in hand, we headed out the plane's exit. The lengthy caterpillar lines that crawled towards the immigration counters didn't deter our jovial mood. I was keen to practise the few Indonesian words hiding under my tongue and air a foreign language from my mouth once again. A fumbling act for me, but funny for the courteous locals.

Then, with passports stamped, we all progressed to the baggage claim carousel. We travelled light. Swimwear, sarongs, sandals, shorts, and smiles were liberally and literally bundled into each bag, now stacked onto two trolleys. The main airport area was full of newly arrived passengers looking for their hotel transport, local drivers waiting with signs and the milling public killing time Balinese style…slowly. We located our transfer minibus assigned to ferry guests to the resort, a half hour drive away. I knew the children were running out of steam but they soon energised, soaking up the hustle and bustle of road life from Denpasar Airport to Nusa Dua. It was an interesting insight into the Bali lifestyle. Traffic of zipping motorbikes overtaking, carrying four astride – man, woman and two kids – was typical.

On arrival at the hotel I left my husband to sort the baggage, then escorted my daughters into the foyer, eager to see our suite, shower, and settle. To greet us, traditional Balinese gamelan music was performed, enhancing the holiday spirit. White painted walls, brown carved wooden furniture, sweet smoky incense, large ceiling fans swirling in whooshes of *come in and cool down*. The resort staff all dressed neatly, wearing warm, genuine hospitality faces, greeted each guest with a refreshing chilled hand-flannel. A pleasant sense of relaxation wrapped around us.

It was wonderful to plonk down into our new lodgings. After an entire day's travelling, the girls were yawning out the last of their liveliness. Bedtime was calling. The luggage was soon room delivered. This allowed for a final count of bags and 'friends'.

The Gift of a Rabbit

Seven bags, check. Youngest daughter with Penny bear, check. Eldest daughter with Gaga rabbit...Oh no! 'Where's Gaga rabbit?' I blurted out.

Yasmin, with eyes meekly downcast, muttered, 'I don't know. I can't find her.'

Panic stations. I hunted around the room. Gaga rabbit was very important. A family member since my daughter was one year old. A gift from my parents. She accompanied us everywhere. In the end, I concluded the worst. We'd left Gaga on the minibus. My imagination took hold to grapple with negative scenarios. This dud super power had not yet developed in my young daughter's mind, thankfully. Battling to keep my composure, I announced I would be back shortly. I needed to go see someone at the front desk. Bewildered eyes watched me leave. Bolting to reception, I promptly revealed the situation about our missing stuffed rabbit. I described her in great detail. Doll size. Wears a flowery jump suit. Yellow ribbon tied to her head. I asked if there was any possibility of searching the vehicle. I was desperate.

'Sorry, Madam. The bus already left. It is delivering other people to their hotels. We'll check with the driver and let you know.'

But I needed more information than that. What was I supposed to tell my daughter? I worried we'd lost Gaga forever, dropped on the roadside or worse still, tossed in a bin somewhere on this foreign island.

'What time does the driver's shift finish? When will he come back to this hotel? Please let me know urgently. The rabbit is my daughter's best friend. We miss her.'

Upon assuring me he'd do all he could to contact the driver, I turned and walked away from the counter. I couldn't contain my grief any longer and sobbed back towards my room. I gave myself a few minutes to pull it together, keyed open the door, and entered. There stood Yasmin, waiting in the living-room next to a side-table where a ceramic lamp sat. Its shaft of light stretched out from its cream shade. The warm glow cast upon Yasmin's blonde curly hair. It shimmered off of her with a halo effect. She looked so angelic, wearing a hopeful expression. I braced myself, then explained the hotel staff were trying to help look for Gaga rabbit. But now it was time to shower, go to bed, and not to worry.

I thought how silly I must have looked with red eyes and how collected my young daughter was. It surprised me. No outburst or tears at her missing best friend. Maybe she saw it her fault for leaving Gaga on the bus, or my error for not doing the usual head count check. Perhaps it was innocent faith. A trust that Gaga was okay, and we'd see her soon. Either way, darkness was upon us and sleep was the only answer.

I tucked my girls into bed and ventured back to reception. The same gentleman informed me the driver wouldn't be at the hotel until midnight. He advised me to try again then. Too tired and emotionally drained, I opted to return first thing in the morning.

That night, I prayed hard. I was unsure if asking for help to find a child's stuffed toy animal was too trivial. All I knew was that the love Yasmin gave her Gaga rabbit morphed that stuffed bunny into a cherished family member. She was irreplaceable. A calming source for my daughter. Gaga offered endless company and support. Losing her was my pain, too. Apprehension set in. Was this the start of how the rest of our holiday was going to play out −

The Gift of a Rabbit

distraught and disappointing? With a heavy mind, my body drifted off to sleep on thoughts of counting hopping bunnies...missing in action.

Early next morning, I dressed quickly and snuck out. Dread still lay on my shoulders. I wondered whether the driver had found anything in his minibus. Once again at reception I enquired about our lost toy rabbit. The receptionist gave me the news. Our soft rabbit had been sitting on the front seat with the bus driver all night. Gaga was a gracious passenger travelling to each stop and returned to the hotel just after midnight. He immediately handed Gaga rabbit to me with a broad smile on his face. With such relief, tears fell like a broken fawcet down my cheeks. Gaga looked at me, speechless. Overwhelmed, all I could utter was 'terima kasih' over and over. Our Gaga had been in caring hands, and I was eternally thankful.

I squashed the life out of Gaga rabbit with hugs all the way back to the room. On entry, I found Yasmin awake. Squeals of excitement escaped her slight frame when she saw who I was holding. I shared the story of how Gaga had started the holiday off early and had a scenic night tour of Bali while we slept. A magical mystery adventure. Our blessed bunny had the pleasure of being chauffeured around before the excursion ended at the hotel, returning to us. Guided back to our hearts. I realised then the powers that be are good and strong and everywhere. With the bond of love and the benefit of prayers, Gaga rabbit made it home safely to her family, where she belonged.

The Vow
Jane Schope

When I said, 'I do' – it was to have and to hold, for better or worse, in sickness and health, for richer, for poorer, from this day forward and forever more. This sacred vow meant everything to me. It was declared to the love of my life in the presence of many witnesses and I meant it with all my heart.

There were many happy times. Life was good, despite a few hiccups along the way. With five children, our home was vibrant, an ever evolving adventure.

Change happened slowly and imperceptibly. I was an obedient, submissive wife and mother of a brood of children. There was little time for reflection. I majored on peace and harmony in the home, little realising my husband was drifting into another reality. In the bad times he reminded me…'You call yourself a Christian, how could you not trust me? Are you forgetting your vow?'

Then disaster struck. One ordinary day a knock on the door changed my life forever. Two policemen asked to see my husband. When he came back in he threw a paper on the floor and screamed: 'It's all lies,' and stormed off down the passage.

I pick it up. I am shaking and feel faint. The charges are listed. I read it over and over in disbelief. How could this be? Offences of which I was totally unaware. This can't be happening.

Fear is haunting me. My eldest son, after reading it, throws himself on his bed and screams: 'I'm going to kill myself.' We cling tightly and weep together.

My husband is released on bail and begins a daily report to the police station.

The Vow

On hearing the news the pastor's wife gently asks: 'How are you feeling?'

'I feel like I'm in a whirlpool. I'm being sucked into the vortex. Round and round I go. I can hardly breathe. I come up for air only to be dragged under again. I think I'm going to drown.'

It is hard to express the devastation. All my dreams, hopes and plans for my family smashed to smithereens. The shame, the embarrassment, the confusion. I feel a tightness in my chest. I wonder if I'm about to have a heart attack. The pain is real. My tears could fill Sydney Harbour. Endless questions in my head. What is happening? Is it my fault? Why didn't I know about it? Simultaneously consumed with guilt, sweltering in anger and tumbling in confusion.

But I have to keep going. Somehow I must focus on my children's needs. Shopping, cooking, cleaning, homework. Life goes on. The mundane continually clashing with the overwhelming. I become an expert actress, pretending all is well with those who do not know, slumping to the floor sobbing as soon as they leave. Now I'm in a fog, what the psychologist called 'psychologically numb – on auto-pilot.'

My husband insists we tell no-one. 'It's all a huge mistake, the less people know about it, the quicker we get our lives back. Remember your vow. We'll get through this if we stick together.'

Then the slow realisation – the depth of his betrayal. The lies. How could he? He hates lies. How could this man I've known for more than forty years have hidden this from me? What an idiot I am! And the confusion. What are the facts? When I dare ask I get gobbledygook. I question my own sanity. I'm reminded again of my vow. Don't ask questions, the less you know the better.

For five years I visit him in prison…sometimes travelling huge distances for a few hours' visit. But there is no change in his attitude. He is adamant he is innocent, despite undeniable evidence and a guilty verdict. Over time he becomes more demanding and irrational. His outbursts are thankfully silenced by the six minute limit on prison phone calls.

Away from him I begin to be more independent and objective. I surprise myself by my assertiveness. I find I can make decisions, actually good ones. Like where we will live, and refusing to accept responsibility for his debts. I am operating a small business with many satisfied clients. I find I am not as incompetent as he kept telling me I was.

I also join Kairos Outside, a ministry supporting women with a family member in prison. Here I find others trying to navigate the horrible challenges of incarceration. It takes a while but, bit by cautious bit, trust begins to grow again. One day I find myself smiling. My face aches as atrophied muscles come back to life.

Finally I see a Christian counsellor. She is compassionate and kind, listening carefully to my story. I know she prays for me before each session and I am so grateful for her wisdom.

At my last session she asks me why I have not divorced. I tell her I am bound by my sacred vow. I promised to stay by my husband through all circumstances, the good times and the bad. I can't divorce him just because we have troubles.

The next few minutes play out in slow motion as I hear my counsellor say: 'But your vow has been irretrievably broken. You are no longer bound by it. Your husband has violated the promises you made together. Even though God hates divorce, there are circumstances in which it is permissible. And in fact, by continuing to support him you are facilitating his wrong-doing and excusing his lies.'

I sit in stunned silence trying to digest what she just said. I carried crippling guilt for so long. He always claimed I was significantly responsible for his failures. 'If you hadn't…If you weren't so…' Surely I was to blame. As a once-close friend viciously told me: 'If you didn't know, you should have known'. It took some time to digest and overcome that accusation.

As I reflected I saw how readily I had excused his anti-social behaviour towards family and friends. I was hiding behind rose-coloured glasses. I couldn't bear to accept the person he really was. What would that say about my judgement over all these years? I loved him. He was the father of my children. We were best friends. Oh really? Do best friends betray you, lie to you and steal your life away?

When I was finally more objective, I was shocked at my own mind games. How could I have been so blind? Was I seriously facilitating his wrongdoing? The thought was crushing.

All too soon our session was over. I left the counsellor's office and jumped on a nearby train. I had about a kilometre to walk home from the station. Without realising it I began to run. When I reached home, panting for breath, I knew the burden had lifted. I was no longer held captive by my vow.

In the next few days I completed divorce papers and, having no assets, no dependent children, and separated by his incarceration, it was easy. The papers were stamped in the courthouse. It was all completed in a few months.

Even though release from my vow lifted a great burden, there was now a different grief. Grief in the finality of my broken marriage and new status with a label. Grief and guilt about any contributing part I played, or how I could have prevented the outcomes. Broken dreams and financial struggles even to this day. Forgiveness doesn't mean reconciliation but it does mean freedom.

Now I have a new vow.

I have vowed to draw ever closer to the One who will never betray me, the One who will never leave or forsake me, who loves me unconditionally. His mercy and forgiveness are new every morning and his faithfulness never fails. He has demonstrated his care and blessings to me in ways I could not have imagined.

Café La Renaissance
Bernice Shen

I love coffee.

Yes, I have to admit I'm something of an addict. I have to have my three cups a day or I can't function. One in the morning with breakfast, one with lunch and one in the afternoon. Every day I go to my local Starbucks and order 'the usual.' I go there so regularly that the barista Nicole knows my name and my order by heart. A short, half-strength, hazelnut latte. No sugar, whipped cream, or chocolate powder on top. My coffee break is my 'me time.' I can zone out and forget about the cares of the world for ten minutes.

I recently started attending a church in the city. Just across from the church is a quaint café called La Renaissance. Every week, as I arrive at church, my bus stops right outside the café.

I would glance through the big latticed windows and see crowds of people inside. One day I saw two men in business suits having their power lunch, hunched over what look like sales figures. On another table an elderly lady was having a tea with her friend. Across from them were two young women deeply engrossed in conversation over a cappuccino. They spoke in hushed tones, but occasionally raised their voices – 'Really?' 'What happened?' They looked like two best friends sharing some big news.

As I looked inside the big windows, I enviously wondered to myself what it would be like for me to have a coffee there. I didn't fancy the thought of going alone though. I didn't want to be the sole patron sitting in the dark corner by myself, quietly sipping coffee while everyone else was in pairs or groups, chatting excitedly to each other. I wanted to be a part of that hustle and bustle. 'God,' I prayed, 'give me an opportunity to have coffee there.'

A few weeks later, I thought nothing of that prayer when I received a call from the church and was invited to join a Bible study group. I had put my name down several months ago and forgotten about it. Sally, the group facilitator, called and introduced herself. 'Would you like to join our new connect group?' she enquired. 'We finally have enough people.'

'I'd love to!' I exclaimed happily. 'Where are we meeting?'

Sally replied, 'La Renaissance.'

We had a delightful Bible study meeting there with six people. There was Stephen, the accountant who had recently emigrated from Indonesia; Paul and Laura, a young married couple; Louise who shared the same taste in films as me, and of course, Sally. 'What will you have?' asked the waiter.

'Short, half-strength, hazelnut latte, please,' I replied. It arrived minutes later, with a beautiful leaf pattern decorating the top. There was that familiar nutty aroma gently scenting the air. Taking that first sip, it tasted every bit as good as it smelt. I had found a new coffee home!

Lessons from Toilet Training
Dienece Darling

There is nothing quite so invigorating as sitting in a chair by lamplight waiting for your toddler to take care of business at almost midnight. At least, my son seems to think so. Weariness drags at every muscle, and some I never even knew existed until I had kids.

'Yeah, Mummy! Some came out,' he whispers with fists pumping in the air. Whispers because the rest of the family are sensibly asleep.

I smile wanly. It does not please my little dictator. After weeks of toilet training, he still can't just go. I must enthusiastically celebrate every successful splashdown. He whines until I paste on a mockingly bright smile, shake my hands in the air like my deaf friends do when they silently applaud each other, follow that with a begrudging thumbs up, and lastly, a lacklustre 'Yeah!' If my toddler understood mockery, he wouldn't be looking at me like I'm the most wonderful person in the world right now.

Boredom trumps the guilt nipping at my conscience. *If only I could read a book or do something while I wait!* But that will muck up the bear of a meticulous routine I accidently created while innocently trying to make toilet training fun. The situation of Mum's chair, the honour of using Mum's super special torch to light his way, and the previously mentioned four ways to celebrate his success are only a fraction of his elaborate night-time toilet routine. How could I have been so mistaken? What I presumed to be temporary trappings have morphed into a settled, draining routine in need of constant new material.

Frustration pulls my head back to the heavens. *God, why do I still have to invent ways to make this interesting? Why can't he just go and be done with it? I mean, I got it when this was new, but it's been months! Shouldn't this just be second nature by now?*

The weirdest concept pops into my head. Is this how God feels when his children are still celebrating things that should be second nature to us by now? Does he get weary when we're stuck on the 'milk of the Word' when we should be chowing down on the 'meat' by now?

Yet you're always gracious to me, God.

My eyes wander back to my son's hopeful face. In the sweet, anxious pleading of his eyes, I see God looking down in grace at me. Determination bolsters my flagging strength. I spread my lips wide in a genuine smile and celebrate enthusiastically with my son. I don't try to skip any steps, and there's not a hint of begrudging or mockery in sight. If God can be gracious when I act like a toddler after being his daughter for years, I can cheer my son until he's ready to conquer the next milestone to growing up.

Thanks for always being gracious and patient with me, God.

The Courage to Go
Anne-Marie Doecke

'Do you think I am an alcoholic?' my father asked me. He had just attended an AA meeting and I had accompanied him. As a pastor, it was particularly difficult for him to acknowledge any problem. I was tentative in my reply and very unsure. Part of me felt that this was a very hard claim to make and part of me did not want to suffer the consequences of feeling disloyal to my father. I could be cast aside and left on my own, and so I remained quiet.

Some years later, as I became more aware of the situation and could no longer deny what was happening, I would sometimes speak to others about it. Rightly or wrongly, there was always a feeling in me that I was betraying the father I loved. I never felt happy talking about him, as it felt so wrong. Once I was told that there are three rules in an alcoholic family, 'Don't trust', 'Don't feel' and 'Don't talk' and I had taken these on board!

Speaking the truth when I was young was far from valued. To survive, I learnt behaviour that focused on people-pleasing and being overly responsible. I often felt when something had gone wrong, that somehow it was my fault. My main focus was on becoming the best person I could be so that nothing bad would happen. This, of course, was a pipe dream!

Mostly unconsciously, I tried so hard to be nice. People would say that I was such a nice person and inwardly I would cringe, because it sounded so insipid and I knew I was not nice all the time. Time after time I was not able to speak the truth, or if I became anxious, I would sometimes lash out at others in an authoritarian way. I wanted to become the person that God wanted me to be, but often felt like I was a failure. I certainly had not been able to save my father.

My father knew about grace. He preached on it in his sermons. My mother knew about grace. She knew God was good but she was brought up in an era when women were expected to obey their husbands. My mother didn't blame my father as she knew he struggled with much inner pain and was in a private hell of his own. Through her own struggles she somehow understood how it was for him, at least in part, and felt compassion for him.

Although my father was able to sustain short periods where he did not touch alcohol, he could not sustain these in the long haul. I remember crying my heart out when I found that he had been drinking again. Eventually, drink took its toll. When he died, I knew that he was at last at peace.

However, within me there remained a deep sense of insecurity and anxiety. My prayers were often for healing for my own inner wounds. I dearly wanted to be the best wife and mother I could be, but felt at times powerless to be who I wanted to be. When I attended church, I wondered where the transformation was happening. I longed for it, yet I knew also that there was something in me that could not understand and even resisted such love.

Early on in my life I had dreamed of becoming an Evangelical sister of Mary. They were an international denominational group of Sisters based in Germany, but who also had a base in Australia. This never eventuated, but sometimes I was able to attend their retreats. The sisters would pray for each participant and put messages under their pillows or at their place at the table. The only message I remember reading was, 'When the bride's heart is ready...' I'm ready now I thought...How can I be more ready?

It was during one of those retreats that I had an unexpected encounter. I was sitting near the front waiting for the speaker to arrive. A lady came from behind and tapped me on the shoulder. I turned in my seat a little but I could not see her face properly. She said, 'I think God wants you to know this: "I did not give you a spirit of timidity but of power and of love and of a sound mind".' She quietly disappeared and I never spoke with her again. I still have no idea who she was.

That verse from Timothy meant so much to me. It seemed like the perfect verse for me. I felt I had so often given away my inner authority. There was also in me a desire to learn to love in a deeper way, one which was not so fear-driven, and I knew I needed self-discipline.

Soon after this experience, I went into what felt like a wilderness time, which lasted for a number of years. My own feelings about myself and my continuing awareness of how I had hurt others led me towards self-destructive behaviour. I often forgot the verse or if I remembered it, would use it to remind myself how far I was from this spirit of love. In desperation, having a mind that was over-active, and often focused on worse case scenarios, I intuitively knew I had no other choice but to begin a practice of silence.

When I found out that the local Anglican Church ran a Christian meditation group, I attended. Here I felt safe. In silence, I could just be as I was. I felt supported by others and could also be supportive without having to use any words. Here, I felt God helped me to let go of ways which left me constantly spinning around myself.

It was when the group could no longer continue at a time when I could participate, that I knew that I had to start my own meditation group. We have now been meeting for around ten years. I would never have believed that I would meditate as I had thought it was non-Christian. It was heartening when I remembered that AA and many other twelve step programs included both prayer and meditation in their eleventh step.

Meditation opened up my life in more ways than I can count. Despite difficulties along the way, I have felt encouraged to continue the practice. For instance, once when I attended a Christian meditation retreat I was given the same verse from Timothy to read. I could not believe it!

When one of my sons wanted to expand my world, and invited me to go overseas and suggested that Singapore would be the perfect place to go, I saw that I had been given a wonderful opportunity. I knew that there were Christian meditation groups there and so I was interested in attending at least a couple of these groups. The hospitality that I was shown, I will never forget. One group was led by a meditator who had been high up in the Singaporean government and who had realised the necessity for silence in his life. To know that leaders were meditating meant a great deal to me.

When I shared my journey with a pastor, he pointed me in the direction of becoming a Benedictine oblate, which is a committed contemplative path. To him, I am forever grateful. I am also grateful to my family for giving me the space to continue my journey. I've had opportunities that I never expected to have had, like being able to contribute a little of my story to a book by Jim Green, *Giving Up Without Giving Up: Meditation and Depressions*.

When I spoke about meditation from a Christian perspective to a mixed religious group, I was then given the opportunity to talk on the community radio program, 'Voices of Faith'. After telling my mother about this, she said to me that my father had also been told that he had a good voice for radio. It made me feel close to him. I have also had the opportunity to attend inter-faith conferences which provide platforms for conversations between different religions. Again, something that I never dreamed I would do.

As an oblate, I recently took part in a meditation retreat online and tears rolled down my face as I saw people young and old from different countries begin to take the contemplative pathway. I believe that we are both Mary and Martha in Scripture and we need to integrate both contemplation and activism in our lives. Stillness may be the basis for action which is truly compassionate and non-violent.

My life has turned out differently from what I expected. It hasn't always been easy, but I have grown in gratitude. God has done for me what I could not do for myself. I have been given, little by little, the desires of my heart and the ability, one baby step at a time, to turn away from many of my persistent, unhelpful thoughts and attitudes. My journey hasn't been understood by everybody but I have been given the courage to go where I never thought I would!

An Old Car and a Hiccough
Jenny Glazebrook

Our car was old. Which wouldn't have mattered except that people knew us as the old-fashioned, religious family who drove the white 'Olden' station wagon with the weird horn. Someone had taken the 'H' off the Holden insignia on the bonnet, and my dad added the Klaxon horn. He took great pleasure in blasting that historic horn at every opportunity.

Mum enjoyed using it, too. I'll never forget the day she dropped me off at high school, skidded the tyres in the gravel outside the gate and gave a quick blast of the Klaxon. It sounded more like a cow hiccoughing than a horn – not that I've ever heard a cow hiccough, but if one did, that's how I imagine it would sound. At the 'Oogah' noise, all my classmates turned to look while I tried to shrink into non-existence.

Then there was the time one of the front wheels on that old car collapsed. We were pulling out onto the road when there was a loud thump. Mum, Dad, my brother, sister and I all got out to find the wheel leaning on a strange angle. Some teenagers around my age stopped to laugh and take photos. Not good when you're shy and at that age where you don't like attention.

That car was forever breaking down. But it was the dramatic breakdown when I was eight that changed my view of life and God forever. It was a hiccough in that Holden's life that prepared me for the biggest hiccough in mine.

It happened one sweltering summer day. We were travelling home from Sydney and we still had hours to go. I was sitting in the back seat with my brother on one side, my sister on the other. I hadn't been well. I'd stopped growing and lost weight in recent months. Being the smallest meant I was expected to sit in the middle even though my brother was two years younger.

As we travelled down the highway, Dad looked over at Mum and said something quietly. Like any normal child, I leaned in to hear whatever the secret might be.

'The fuel is getting very low.'

Dad's words made my heart quicken. We'd been stuck in this car before, waiting for help or roadside assistance. But what would happen if we were stuck in the middle of nowhere in this heat with no fuel?

I began to pray. 'Please God, please, please let there be a petrol station soon.'

I was an anxious child and so my prayers turned into silent begging. I was desperately hot, thirsty and needing the toilet. In those days, many service stations weren't open on Sundays. We needed a miracle.

'There's one.' Mum was pointing up ahead to a beautiful sight. A blue and white sign indicating a petrol station.

'Thank you God,' I breathed.

'It might not be open,' Dad warned as he pulled in.

'Please God,' I begged silently. 'Please, please let it be open so we can get petrol.'

Mum sighed. 'It's closed.'

And my heart sank.

Why? God was supposed to be able to do anything. I'd heard all the Bible stories about his amazing miracles in the past. Daniel in the lion's den. Moses in the wilderness. Jesus healing people. Why wouldn't God answer my simple prayer and let the petrol station be open so we could get home? I shuffled uncomfortably, my skin sticking to the vinyl seat. I was tired of this heat.

As we pulled back onto the highway, all was silent in the car. I was discouraged and disillusioned. Maybe God didn't hear my prayers. Maybe he didn't care about me. I was too small and insignificant.

'I don't know how much further we'll get,' Dad said as the car built up speed again. 'We're almost out.'

Mum sat up straight, her head tilted to the side. 'What's that noise?'

I strained my ears to listen.

'Can you hear that kind of chain, rattly noise?' she asked Dad.

I could. I tensed. What was it?

Mum had commented on a worrying whirring sound in one of the car's wheels over the past weeks, but this was something different altogether.

Without warning the car jerked sideways with a loud crack. It leaned at a precarious angle, throwing me against my brother. A horrible scraping noise filled my ears as we skidded along the road. I jerked my head around to look out the back window. It looked as though autumn leaves were streaming from the back of the car. But it was sparks. And one of our wheels was flying across the other side of the highway. It spiralled one last time and came to rest in some long, dry grass.

Dad maneuvered the car to the side of the road and we all sat in stunned silence. A man travelling the other direction skidded to a stop and grabbed something from his car. A blanket. The wheel had set some grass alight and flames were roaring to life. He desperately beat them with the blanket.

Dad was the first to jump out of our car, followed by Mum. I sat frozen in shock, heart pounding.

'What happened?' my brother asked, eyes wide.

Mum opened the back door and helped him undo his seatbelt. 'The wheel came off. You can all come out, but make sure you stand away from the road.'

I climbed out on shaky legs, feeling sick, my mouth dry. I needed a drink more desperately than ever. My heart was still pounding as I followed Mum down the small embankment beside our car. There was a strange smell. Rubber? Petrol? Burning? Dad was over the other side of the road talking with the man who had managed to beat out the flames.

'I need the toilet,' I told Mum.

She was sympathetic. 'Sometimes a fright can do that.'

I held on, anxious and uncomfortable. Why had this happened?

We waited beside our forlorn, lopsided car until a tow truck arrived.

The burly tow truck driver bent to look under the car. 'Your wheel bearings collapsed. The axle was scraping along the road. It's put a hole in your petrol tank.'

We watched as the car was loaded onto the tow truck. My brother and sister shared fascinated excitement, but I was scared. What if the car slipped and fell off the truck as the chains pulled it on? What if we couldn't get home?

Our white 'Olden' looked small on the back of that big tow truck. We piled into the truck. Mum and Dad in the front with the driver and the three of us children in the back.

'You're lucky,' I heard the burly tow truck driver say to Dad. 'There's a huge hole in your petrol tank and if you'd had petrol in there...'

I leaned forward to hear better.

'The same thing happened to another vehicle recently,' he told Dad as we bumped along the highway. 'But his petrol tank was full. The car exploded.' He shot Dad a sideways look. 'Someone up there must be looking after you.'

The words sank in. If the petrol station had been open as I had prayed it would be, our petrol tank would have been full...and with all those sparks...

As we arrived closer to town, the driver pointed to a blackened, burnt out paddock. 'That's from the car that exploded.'

It was then I knew. God had known best all along. He hadn't ignored my prayers. He'd said 'No' because he cared. To preserve my life.

The truth was almost more than I could take in.

My grandparents came to take us all home while the old Holden undertook massive repairs.

That same year I was diagnosed with an incurable disease. My weight loss and thirst were all symptoms of the auto-immune condition, type 1 diabetes. I was terrified of needles, but now I would be having them every day of my life. I hated being different, standing out, but it was more than an old car with a Klaxon horn that made me different, now.

And so I begged God to take away the diabetes. To heal me.

He didn't. But I knew deep in my heart that he wasn't ignoring me. He has allowed me to have diabetes because he can use me like this and bring Jesus glory through it.

God used that hiccough in my young life to show me his saving power. He knew what was coming. He knew I needed to realise that when he says 'no', it's because he knows best; he sees the big picture and knows what is coming. I now know that every hiccough in my life is part of his perfect plan.

Proude by Name, House-proud by Nature
Ai Mee Ling

I was very unhappy but what should I do? Since arriving in Adelaide in March on a scholarship, I had been boarding with Miss D, a retired nurse. My room was very comfortable, and the food was decent. However, she frowned about friends visiting, said that I must be very dirty because I showered twice a day, and about my packed lunch: 'Bread and butter is OK. Bread, butter and jam is good. Bread, butter, jam and a slice of cheese is simply ridiculous!' But what irked her most was my study habits. In Malaysia, I grew up in a rubber estate, post-World War II, where the generator ran from 3am to 7am and from 6 to 9pm daily. I developed the lifelong habit whereby my best hours of concentrated study were before dawn. But here in Adelaide, Miss D would open my room door while I was studying at 3am, switch off the heater and light, all the while muttering, 'Nonsense. Peculiar. Madness'. She was a light sleeper and my desk light and studying in the early hours disturbed her sleep. I started to pray that if I was to move, the Lord would provide.

By mid-November, exams were finished. Over Christmas, I got a job at David Jones. To my delight, I was assigned to 'Books & Stationery', my favourite department. Wrapping books was easy, and during lull periods, I could read from books and open selected ones for browsing – otherwise how was I to recommend good books to shoppers?

Around mid-December, a dear old lady came by and asked for my help. She wanted to buy a significant present for her student boarder, Emmanuel, who had just completed medical school. I took her through various options, before she finally settled on a Parker ball-point pen. As I wrapped it up, she started to sniff, and then to cry into her handkerchief. She would miss Emmanuel, who had boarded with her five years! As she walked away, I thought to myself, 'What a funny old thing!' Within ten minutes she came back and asked for me. I thought she wanted to exchange the purchase or complain about me.

'Dearie, do you have a place to stay?' she asked.

'Yes,' I replied.

'You look like a very nice student. If you are looking for a place to board, I have a room now that Emmanuel is leaving.' She wrote out her name – Ada Rose Proude – and her telephone number, and left. I put the paper away and carried on working.

I forgot about the incident until the weekend when I was praying and again asked the Lord, 'Lord, please show me if I am to move and provide me with a good home.'

'I have already given you a place,' he said.

'What? That peculiar old lady!' I said.

'Yes.'

Because of this, I phoned Mrs Proude to tell her that after 24 December, I would have finished my job at David Jones but would be going to Brisbane on 26 December to attend the Overseas Christian Fellowship convention at King's College, University of Queensland, and that I would not be back till after mid-January.

On the second day of convention, I heard an announcement over the PA system, 'Ling Ai Mee, you have mail.' To my surprise, I found it was a postcard from Mrs Proude. In childish squiggly writing she wished me 'Merry Christmas' and suggested that I visit her and see the room when I returned to Adelaide. She lived in Croydon, an old inner-city suburb of Adelaide, neighbouring the railway station. Croydon was poorer than the outer suburbs; the nouveau riche preferred the eastern hill suburbs or by the beach.

When I got back to Adelaide, I knew it was time for the visit and silently hoped that Mrs Proude would have found someone in the two weeks I was away. I was also a bit afraid, so I asked Peter Cheng, a Hong Kong dental post-grad student, to take me. Peter had an old beat-up grey Vauxhall Wyvern and we slowly drove along Hawker Street looking for the correct house number. The houses on both sides were quite old and some were not well kept. We passed a new, pretty one and kept driving on. When we realised that we had missed it, we turned back. The house was the pretty house with a lovely front garden.

We knocked at the door and Mrs Proude met us and took us through the house, past the master bedroom reserved for guests, the second bedroom which she used, right to the small back bedroom which she was letting out, a sun-room off the laundry area. The house was immaculately clean and tidy. She was Proude by name and house-proud by nature. The sun-room was much smaller than the one I had at Miss D's, but she said I could have use of the kitchen if there were friends visiting. Her sitting and dining rooms were also for special guests. The rent was ten shillings less a week. I had prayed, so I said 'yes' to the Lord's provision. When I went back to Miss D, she gave me an earful, warnings of 'odd bods and dangerous places.'

I moved just before term started. Mrs Proude's house was on the bus route, a convenient ride and walk to get to uni. Mrs Proude cooked dinner and packed my lunch for me. On the first Saturday she called out that she was turning on the washing machine and did I have washing? I had not expected laundry service! I stayed with Mrs Proude for the rest of my time at uni. When I had to stay late at uni, she would give me two shillings for a pie and soup dinner, and when I got back she would have a light dinner or stew waiting. To top it all, she would count the times I would spend with friends for dinner, especially my Aussie friends, and she then would tell me it was time to reciprocate their hospitality. She would then give me money to buy meat and groceries from Tom the Grocers, a 300m walk from the house, and I would prepare and cook an Asian dinner and invite two or three Aussie friends home. I now had a home to invite friends to.

Eventually, she also came to Overseas Christian Fellowship meetings once or twice a month. She then asked me to invite my Asian friends home for meetings. We used her living room and later her dining room as well. Soon the whole house was open for my use and for occasional OCF meetings. I believe she had a personal experience of the Lord during those OCF years. She had always professed she was a Christian. When I bought a car in my final Honours year, Mrs Proude thoroughly cleaned out the garage that she had used as a storeroom. Every evening, she would wait in the garden and open the gate and garage door when I returned in my little beige car.

Mrs Proude had never finished primary school. She had been sent to house-keep for Mr Proude, a middle-aged bachelor farmer in Port Lincoln. Eventually they fell in love and married. He died of stomach troubles and left her with the farm and funds for life. She built this cute cottage in Croydon to live in. Why in poor

Croydon? She had lived and grown up there and had friends there, and her older sister was also staying in Hawker Street.

After graduating as a biochemist, I eventually settled in Singapore. Mrs Proude never visited me as she was afraid of flying. But we corresponded regularly and I sent her photos of my wedding and especially of the children when they came. When I won return tickets to Australia, I took my children, aged seven and five, for a holiday in December. We visited Mrs Proude and saw that she had hung my children's photos in her living room and above the fireplace. In the garden, she removed the old lace table cloths that covered the grape vines and fruit trees to keep away the birds. My two kids had the time of their life picking grapes and climbing the tree to pick yummy peaches. Five years later, we visited her again and my mother came with us this time. That was my last visit to Mrs Proude. She died a few years after.

One day I received a packet parcel in the post. It was from her niece and it contained all the photos I had sent Mrs Proude, which she had lovingly preserved, sharing them with her family who visited. I also received a letter from her lawyers telling me that Mrs Proude had endowed each of my two children with AUD500, to be received when they turned eighteen. Mrs Proude loved us. We were 'family'! I do miss Mrs Proude.

Finding God on the Streets
Ruth C. Hall

'John! We never thought you'd make it, mate!'
John stared back at Gary. As the meaning sank in, it shocked him to the core. He thought he'd fooled them all that time, that he'd kept the pain and despair to himself. It wasn't something he'd wanted them or anyone to know.

Bumping into Gary was amazing after all these years. A casual visit to a friend's church and there he was. They'd been through a lot together nearly two decades ago, so catching up was a good thing. But now, finding out that Gary and other staff at the homeless centre had thought John was one of those who would not 'make it' was actually quite confronting.

Talking more with his old friend, he realised that somehow they must have seen the depth of anguish that plagued his troubled mind at that time. But the John that Gary knew back then was very different to this small-business owner with a nice home and steady relationship that stood before him today.

At forty-three years old and with a successful life behind him, John had been calling the streets of Adelaide home for twelve months on first meeting Gary. He lived rough, looked rough and smelled rough. By this time he had discovered his own hiding places around the city where he could withdraw and feel reasonably safe overnight. Not mixing with other homeless people, he rarely made use of the overnight shelters offered to those living on the streets. John became very good at scrounging for food and knew when and where the different meals were offered by charities. Walking for many miles each day he got to know every crack and weed in the city streets and lanes. He walked with his head down, discouraging any eye contact with everyday people. Not into drugs or alcohol, or even smoking, he was a bit of an enigma in street-life.

Being highly intelligent, with an over-active and often racing mind, one of the hardest aspects of living this way was filling the empty days. John's previous life had been full and often hectic. But what do you do when you have nothing to do, with long hours, days and weeks to do it in? He had to feed his mind; sometimes it was all that kept him on the right side of madness. He would scavenge newspapers and magazines from bins and filled many notebooks with writings.

Keeping safe and protected from the bad street-elements also took a lot of thought and energy. He became quite preoccupied with the daily planning and procedure of finding a safe and dry sleeping place, not settling into the chosen spot until well after dark when there was less chance of being seen. He had a few favourite bushes and out-of-the-way hide-outs, but made sure he varied them regularly. If others knew where he was sleeping, he could be at risk of harm.

Friday and Saturday nights were the hardest. Why did the homeless seem to bring out the worst in everyday people? He was spat on, yelled at, pushed, kicked and even urinated on as he would sit sheltered in doorways on the cold and rainy nights when it was particularly hard to find shelter.

He'd found out the hard way that there were brutal and cruel people around. A few weeks after finding himself on the streets, sleeping under a bench in a city park, he'd been beaten and attacked in the worst possible way by a group of men. After that, the breakdown that led him to be living this way quickly developed into anxiety and severe panic attacks.

John would often think back over his life before the streets. He'd grown up in Barmera, a small country town a few hours north-east of Adelaide. Having a carefree, though strict Catholic upbringing with siblings and parents who loved him and a broad extended family, he'd left school to work in the railways. What a life he'd led! Working as a train driver before becoming a successful ABC sports and political journalist and commentator, life was demanding. Achieving high acclaim as a football umpire and a sought after race-caller, he married, had a son and was living life to the full in Darwin.

With a mischievous sense of humour and strong family focus, John had always been a hard worker and perfectionist but suddenly it all came crashing down. His marriage failed, then work began to fall apart and he experienced what later would be described as a mental breakdown. A typical country man of that era, he'd prided himself on being strong, or so he thought. Men were tough, they just got on with it. Sure there was lots of stress, but he'd been dealing with it. Until all of a sudden he just couldn't anymore.

Sinking, floundering in quicksand, he had no idea what to do. So he went to Adelaide, ran out of money, started sleeping out rough, and just stayed that way. There were family he could have gone to, but somehow that didn't seem an option. John himself didn't understand what was happening to him, so how could his loved ones? Confused and alone, he'd lost control of his life. How could he put this burden on his family and friends?

John was to live this way for nearly a decade. Finding it hard to be in closed rooms, especially with a certain type of man, he would be highly vigilant, always calculating a way out of any situation or building. In the beginning he trusted no one and was constantly on the alert to protect himself, living a life of fear with the daily focus being on survival. For the first few years of street living, life was very controlled by his anxiety, deep depression and debilitating panic attacks.

Later, John was to learn that undiagnosed Asperger's contributed to him being unable to move from his self-imposed street life. This condition meant that he actually become good at this life; it had become addictive, and it was hard to break the cycle. He survived by just living one day at a time.

During this time he used to visit some of the mobile meal services that would set up tables and chairs and serve from their vans. While the hot meals were much appreciated, he wasn't interested in talking to anyone. In fact he discouraged any type of connection. They were nice enough people, and they meant well, but he would take his meal and sit as far away from any others as he could. Sometimes the workers would try to start a conversation but without being rude, John just did not engage with them.

One of these was run by Coastlands Church. John wasn't at all interested in church or religion. Although respecting his Catholic upbringing which included being an altar boy for ten years and seven years at a convent school run by nuns, it seemed to have no relevance to life as an adult. He went for the meals most weeks though, and over time started seeing something different about these people. They respected his desire not to chat and were just happy to provide a meal, a friendly smile and some encouraging words. They didn't push any agenda, which helped him to slowly feel more relaxed. It took around a year, but eventually John found himself responding more and more.

About this time he started visiting the Teen Challenge venue in the city centre – initially for food and a meal, not realising it was anything to do with God. The leader, Morrie, was someone John felt drawn to. He didn't push any of them: homeless, alcoholics and druggies, it didn't matter, he simply accepted each person. Just giving of himself, and whatever he had, to help.

Gary, Morrie, the Coastlands and Teen Challenge workers – these Christians showed God's love to John without pushing it on him. Almost as if they were there just to love people, allowing God to initiate any changes. Somehow these people were different.

This connection and acceptance was the beginning of change for John. It was not immediate and happened over several years. But it did happen. Feeling God's love through these people was the beginning of a newfound walk with his heavenly Father. It was a long journey for John but he gradually began to heal and was able to move from the streets to a small home unit, start a small business and reconnect with family and friends.

Meeting Gary all these years later reminded him of how far he'd come. It seemed even the workers who dealt with homeless people had not believed he would make it. But looking back, even when his life was shattered and broken, and he'd been at his lowest, John realised that he had never actually been alone. God had always had his hand on John.

The Sound of Children Playing
May-Kuan Lim

'I'm sorry but you can't bring your daughter to class,' said my head teacher.

'Please, please,' pleaded the mother, 'I couldn't organise childcare for today.'

The little girl in question, frizzy hair pulled back in two pigtails, looked up at her mother, and started pushing at the head teacher's knees, as if trying to push away her mother's source of distress. But the vocational college had a strict 'No Children' rule, and my head teacher and I had no choice but to enforce college rules. So, the young mother gathered her books and left with daughter in tow.

The student had come to Australia from Africa, and was in my class to learn computing and English. I empathised with her. I had once been a young mother myself, and had felt opportunities passing me by while I was at home caring for my young children. Around a third of my students were young mothers. They would rush into class after drop-off, and sometimes had to leave early if a child was sick at home. I realised that the young mothers in my class represented many more young women at home who had no viable childcare options.

One Sunday in church I was lining up for lunch with Phoebe, one of our Mainly Music leaders, and Melvin, our Community Outreach pastor. Melvin had been looking for a way to serve the community in one of Adelaide's inner-city suburbs. I shared how I felt that children should not be viewed as a hindrance to adult learning, especially with languages, because young children pick up new languages effortlessly. The three of us started talking about whether mothers and their pre-schoolers could learn English together. The idea struck a chord with Phoebe. We decided to run a weekly session for mothers and their children to learn English together in a private home of one of our church members.

Every Friday for the next few months, Phoebe would lug her computer and puppets and shakers and other such props to the small three-bedroom old brick house. We pushed back the sofa to make more room. We projected colourful slides onto the living room wall. With our shoes left at the door, we would sit cross-legged on the carpet, singing and clapping. Then the adults would step over toys and children, to another room, where I taught an English lesson while Phoebe looked after the children. After half-an-hour, or till the children wanted their mothers, we would adjourn to the kitchen for a cup of Persian tea.

We taught conversational English and printed out worksheets. We sang about animals and rainbows, boats and body parts. But for many activities there was no room. It was too cramped. We brainstormed. How could we get more space – reclaim the overgrown garden? Clean out the shed? Meanwhile, Melvin and others would walk around the neighbourhood praying, talking to the people they met. Eventually, Melvin went to the council's Community Centre. It turned out that the centre coordinator had been looking for a program to cater for pre-school children. Phoebe, Melvin and I went to meet her, and she showed us around the centre, showing us which rooms were available. The ideal room – mid-sized, with a projector and carpet – had already been taken, so she said we could use the gymnasium. The acoustics were poor, and lighting less than ideal for a projector, but it was a large, and it was available. So we agreed that we would start running classes the following year. Phoebe registered us with Mainly Music, and Shereleen and Kai joined our core team.

We began in February 2020 with just two regular families, a mother and her daughter, and a grandmother and her grandson. A couple more families joined soon after. They had heard about us through our flyer drop and the Community Centre advertisement.

    Not long after, a lady from our church met a group of mothers and their young children in the nearby playground and invited them to the program. Although they lived nearby, they had never ventured inside the Community Centre. Culturally it was not the norm for women to mix freely with men whom they were not related to. Furthermore, they were a people who had suffered years of war and trauma, and it was hard for them to trust strangers. With a little encouragement one or two mothers came along with their young children. And they kept coming because the mothers loved the opportunity to catch up over morning tea, and the children loved the music:

    Knees, knees, clap
    You are a star
    Please let me tell you what a blessing you are
    Knees, knees, clap
    Clap hands with me
    I am so thankful that you're on my team.

There was something joyous about these simple lyrics. I found myself looking forward to Fridays. As the weeks passed, we could see that the regular children loved coming. A few of the little girls would take the trouble to dress up, and were thrilled when we noticed their special outfits. Others would run up to us when they came or give us a hug before they left. When I bent down to help them choose stickers, or dance along to the songs, I would be reminded of the days when my children were very young, when I shared their world of simple joys.

In time, a social worker from a neighbouring school heard about our group, and started directing families to us. She even came along to make sure that they were settling in well to our program. Our church community rallied around the program and we soon had a core team of volunteers with people bringing morning tea, helping with registration and nametags, equipment set-up and songs, serving and washing up. COVID brought things to a halt temporarily, but when we resumed the program, we found that the other community groups with whom we had previously shared the space seemed to have disbanded. As a result, we had the whole gymnasium to ourselves, and the children found great joy in playing catch or riding toy bikes and cars round and round while their mums and carers sat around tables with cups of tea. The centre coordinator herself even popped in to see us most weeks.

I remember an occasion during the past year when, in my Bible reading plan, I came to Zechariah chapter seven. I was struck by the words, 'This is what the Lord Almighty says: 'Once again men and women of ripe old age will sit in the streets of Jerusalem, each with cane in hand because of his age. The city streets will be filled with boys and girls playing there.'

As I meditated on these words, images of painted butterflies on the walls of the Community Centre, the songs and the music came back to me. I thought of how the rainbow had been given as a symbol of hope to humanity. I felt that God was giving us a promise too, and that we should use these verses as a basis for prayer. I shared this with the others, and we prayed that the streets of this suburb would be filled with the sounds of children playing, and that aged men and women would be able to enjoy these sounds of joy.

In September 2020, we participated in Community Day organised by the centre coordinator. Our church helped to supply food and drinks, supervise the bouncy castle and mini-golf, operate a mobile green-screen photography space, and do face painting and henna painting. We ran a Mainly Music session celebrating Father's Day. That day, the Community Centre was overflowing with people, grandparents with walking canes, parents with their children, many who knew us. We were all struck by the joy on the children's faces. We left exhausted, but buoyed by the sounds of children playing. It felt like the beginning of the fulfilment of God's promise.

Birthday Catalyst
Boo Hooi Jimmy Khoo

As I lay down in my hospital gown looking up at the ceiling, I thought back to seven months earlier.

Seven months ago on my birthday I decided to do something different by signing up for introductory ice-skating classes with my children. On that evening we all had a wonderful time, with the exception of me, having had a couple of hard falls.

Months later and I found myself with my GP trying to figure out the numbness in my left foot. I thought the numbness and tingling were due to the fall, that it was something more serious than the tailbone soreness I experienced for weeks after the fall. With suspicions pointing towards coccyx tailbone and lumbar region injuries, we made arrangements for a lumbar region MRI scan. However, I also pointed out that I might have been imagining a burning sensation up in my left abdomen area. In the end we decided to have the whole spinal cord scanned instead.

The day for the MRI scan came and I spent almost two hours at the imaging centre instead of the planned forty minutes. I didn't give it any thought until I saw my GP two weeks later, on a Monday. I received the devastating news. On that fateful afternoon, I remember vividly that my GP told me that I had a lesion in my T6/7 spinal cord. It was a surprise find as the lesion was found in the spinal cord up near my chest region instead of the lower lumbar region. I decided to call my wife after I left the medical centre and break the news to her. Through her voice, I sensed that she was concerned but calm.

As my GP appointment was during my work lunch time, I slowly drove back to my office to pack up my things. I had to excuse myself from work for the rest of the day. My drive home was a long one. It was during this time that I felt the seriousness of my situation. I was so sick to my stomach. I had difficulty focusing on the road. There were so many thoughts and questions going through my mind. There was this dreadful fear of paralysis. What if the lesion is malignant? What's going to happen to my wife and children? How much will our lives be affected?

I decided to pull over to the side of road and take a breather. After I regained my composure, I contacted two of my close friends who are medical professionals to ask them to review my MRI report and recommend a neurologist who could see me quickly. In the next few days, armed with a list of neurosurgeons, I frantically made phone calls to get an appointment. I was informed by the staff that I needed to provide my GP referral and MRI report for triage before an appointment can be arranged. I called the neurosurgeon clinic again the next day to follow up on my case triage. I was frustrated that I was not in control of the situation. I couldn't even get a date for an appointment.

Out of the blue, on Friday evening, I received a call informing me that an appointment had been set for the following Friday for me to see a specialist. Hallelujah, our prayer had been answered.

Friday came and my wife and I were sitting anxiously outside the specialist's office. By the time we both met the neurosurgeon, we realised that God had gone before us and arranged a very considerate and gentle neurosurgeon to meet us. At the end of the consult, all our questions were answered. My surgery date was set for the following Monday. The good news was that the risk of paralysis from the surgery was zero percent.

Over the weekend I reflected on my journey. I realised that I was very much at peace. I felt very grateful that we found the lesion. It could have continued to grow. In the worst possible situation, I may be paralysed if the lesion damaged my spinal cord. I was grateful that I had the support of my family, friends, and church community. I was grateful that God put me in the good hands of such a good surgeon and his team of medical professionals. I was so much at peace that when the admission ward nurse called to confirm my surgery details, I told her that I looked forward to the surgery. She sounded very surprised. She told me that it was the first time she had a patient who was looking forward to surgery.

The day of the surgery arrived. It was a wet morning when we left home for the hospital. There was silence in the car, but it was the calm and peaceful kind of silence as we slowly made our trip into the city. By the time I was wheeled into the operating theatre, I said my prayers and had fully surrendered to God. Everything was a blur after that.

I woke up in ICU surrounded by beeping sounds. There were tubes coming out of both my hands, back and lower body. On the first night after the surgery, under the influence of heavy pain relief drugs coupled with residual anaesthetics, I threw up. I was also in a lot of pain. I dared not move at all while lying in bed and kept on pressing the pain relief dispenser button. I had to hold my breath when the nurses turned me over to check on my wound. I called out to God and he comforted me through the night.

Over the next five days, I was so reliant on my faith in God for all the nights that I went through. From the times at 3 a.m. when I woke up in cold sweats with pain around my wound, to the nights when I couldn't find the best position to sleep without numbness in my lower left side. I learned to be still and allowed God to be with me and carry me through everything in my prayers. These were also the moments that I used to glorify God by sharing God's words on my social media page for my friends and families.

It was also comforting to know that our church community was rallying behind us with prayer chains during my surgery and providing emotional and logistical support to my wife and two boys.

As I come back to this present moment in my ward, my rehab journey has just begun. I may be in pain. My rehabilitation may take months. I will have to work on my balance and learn to walk again. There is so much uncertainty surrounding my recovery process, but I do know one thing for sure. I am at peace. God is here with me on my journey. He took away the lesion in my back, helped me with clarity in my life priorities, made me cherish my family and friends and ultimately allowed me to surrender to him in my most vulnerable period. God has given me my best birthday gift. My birthday fall was the catalyst for God's transformation work in my life.

Life is Precious
Jenelle Francis

In November 1997 I was diagnosed with bowel cancer, which required major surgery. I was told my prognosis was bleak as my lymph nodes were infected and I would need to have chemotherapy as well. But I had no intention of having chemotherapy. I believed that if the Lord was calling me home and it was my time, then I should not fight him.

My family and surgeon were unhappy with my attitude. I kept telling them that we are all going to die one day and that I was going to a better place. I couldn't understand why they were giving me such a hard time.

I was still in hospital in Sydney when my pastor phoned me. After I had told him of my decision not to have chemo he asked if he could pray with me. I said I would like that very much. There were a lot of visitors in my room at the time, and I could barely hear him, but I remember that he prayed that the Lord would help me to make this major decision.

Now I was not on any medications at the time as I was allergic to morphine and other pain medications, so my mind was very clear.

About two hours after my pastor prayed with me and all my visitors had gone, I was watching golf on television when suddenly everything around me went white and it was as if the television was no longer there. A voice spoke to me from above and said, 'Life is precious.' I shook my head in amazement and asked, 'Where did that come from?' After a pause the voice continued, '…and I gave it to you,' I sank down in my bed and prayed to God, asking forgiveness for not valuing my life enough to fight for it.

When I returned to my home in Port Macquarie I contacted the pastor who had prayed for me to tell him of my amazing experience. He did not seem surprised at all as he hears from God all the time. I had thought God only spoke to Moses and those other people in the Old Testament.

The pastor suggested that I attend the healing services held at St Thomas' church. I had never been to a healing service before and didn't know what to expect. During these services many prayers were said by me and on my behalf. I was convinced that God had healed me. I felt so well.

My doctors, however, arranged for me to have blood tests in preparation for chemotherapy. But I felt that God had already healed me through prayer. If I went ahead with chemo would that mean I didn't have faith in God's healing? So I prayed and asked God, 'Why am I taking chemotherapy when I believe you have healed me? I feel like a hypocrite and you will think that I have no faith after all the prayers I have had.'

On my way home from the first blood test my husband decided to tell me a joke. I was not in any mood for humour, but a felt a voice telling me, 'Be a good wife and listen.'

So my husband began:

'There was a flood and a boat was sent to rescue a man who was stranded. He refused to get in the boat, saying, "I have faith in the Lord and he will rescue me." A couple of hours later another boat was sent to rescue the man and once again he refused to get in, saying, "I have faith that God will rescue me." Now the floodwaters had risen and the man was on his roof so they sent a helicopter to rescue him. Once again, he refused – and drowned. When he arrived in heaven he said, "Lord, what am I doing here? I had faith that you would rescue me." And God said, "Well, I sent two boats and a helicopter."'

When my husband finished the story I burst out: 'So God does have a sense of humour.'

And once more a voice came to me from above, and there was laughter in the voice as God said to me: 'I'm sending you to chemo. Now take it.'

I heard God's audible voice and received his grace and healing through chemo. That was my miracle.

Planes, Cars and God's Intervention
Ivan Francis

There were two times in my life in which God intervened. If he had not, I would not be here today. The first time was in late November 1961. I was on a plane from the US to Australia wondering what lay ahead for me. The company I had been working for had been bought out, and my division wound down. So I accepted a position with another computer company that had just received a major order from Canberra. They needed experienced people for the installation. So I found myself bound for a country where I knew no one, employed by a company where I knew no one, and with only a cursory knowledge of the equipment for which I was now the expert. But I was young, single and fearless.

Now the flights in those day were a lot longer than the fifteen plus hours of today. But due to a strong tail wind we arrived in Sydney earlier than scheduled. Then the interventions of God began. The earlier flight to Canberra has been delayed, so combined with my early arrival, I was put onto the earlier flight that was just boarding so that I would be spared a three hour layover. I arrived exhausted in Canberra and slept most of the next day. Just after five in the afternoon I came down to the lobby to meet with other representatives of my company. But first I went to the reception desk and had a chat with a very attractive young woman at the counter. Her name was Jenelle. We have now been married for fifty-seven years! I then purchased the evening paper, and on the front page saw the photo of the tail of an Ansett-ANA airplane sticking out of the water of Botany Bay. It was the flight I was scheduled to be on. Sadly, there were no survivors. It was one of Australia's worst aviation disasters. I had been in Australia for

Planes, Cars and God's Intervention

only a few hour hours, had met my future wife, and avoided certain death due to tailwinds and a delayed previous flight to Canberra.

But God was not done intervening. In 1982 I lost my leg, and nearly my life.

It was Easter Sunday and we were returning home from our holiday house in the Pocono mountains of Pennsylvania. There had been a late snow fall and as our daughter had been driving for only eight months I thought it would be good for her to gain experience driving in the snow. She did a beautiful job of pulling up in front of our garage. I got out to unlock the garage door, but it was dark and I had my wife's keys so I had trouble finding the right key. My wife got out of the car to help me, using the headlights from the car. The car was on a slant and began to roll. When this happened our daughter went to brake but hit the accelerator instead. As the car lurched forward she pushed down even harder on the accelerator, still thinking it was the brake. My wife Jenelle was able to jump out of the way, but I was not. The car went through the garage door and pinned me against the cinderblock wall at the back of the garage.

After the accident there were five events that I can only view as God's intervention. Our daughter ran inside the house to call an ambulance while Jenelle tried to apply a tourniquet on my badly injured leg with her jacket. After that she ran across the street to a neighbour to ask for help. She opened their front door and ran in screaming for help. The neighbour was stunned as he had just dead bolted the door. But Jenelle was able to run straight in and seek help. That was the first intervention.

The first help to arrive was a fireman who was able to apply a proper tourniquet, slowing the loss of blood. We lived about three miles from a volunteer fire station that was only staffed when a fire call came in. They had received a call earlier which turned out to be a false alarm so they were still at the station when they heard our daughter's call to the ambulance over their monitoring system. That was the second intervention.

The ambulance soon arrived and the race to the hospital began. I had lost a lot of blood and was fading in and out of consciousness. A local surgeon was on his way home, had heard the distress call, and flagged down the ambulance, providing further help. This was the third intervention.

The hospital was on the other side of town. Jenelle was in a car following the ambulance and told me that there was a policeman at each traffic light stopping all traffic to ensure the ambulance was not delayed. We have never seen that happen before or since in that town. This was the fourth intervention.

At some point when they were working on me at hospital I died and they had to resuscitate me. This was the fifth intervention.

I turn 88 this year and as I reflect over the many years back to these events I wonder why I was saved. The amazing number of things that occurred in each instance could not have been simple luck. And I do not believe in mass coincidences. But I do know that since these events I have tried to use my time for God. I have been much more active in church life. I completed an advanced diploma in theology which allowed me to lead services in nursing homes for many years, among other activities. I often recall Romans 7:24 'What a wretched man I am! Who will rescue me from this body of death? Thanks be to God through Jesus Christ our Lord!'

I Wrote a Poem about It
Claire Bell

I have never known the death of an elderly relative except as a rumour from the other side of an ocean. My parents have not yet passed away, but nothing prepared me for both of them developing dementia in their eighties. To me, the loss of parents while they are still alive is a kind of death.

I am the only living child in my family. When our children were young we moved to Adelaide to be near my parents in their old age. At that stage they were more support to us than we were to them, and the proximity of their family was a joy they had not counted on.

Our children grew up, the girls married, and we all tried to continue regular family time with my parents. Once my mother lost her independence after a particularly bad fall, Dad became her carer. The dynamics shifted as Mum adapted to her change of status and limited capacities. These were difficult years which led subtly into the beginnings of dementia.

One day on my weekly visit to their home, I was chatting away to Mum as usual when she picked up a book and started to read as if I were not there. It was a complete shock to see her do this. She had always been a very engaged and patient listener. This was not my mum.

I did not know how to manage my feelings as this pit of horror and grief opened up before me. So I wrote a poem about it, spilling my pain onto paper.

That was the first day I felt I had lost my mother, the first day I saw clearly how many ways she was changing and becoming less like herself. She was quick enough to point out that Dad's memory and confused thinking were probably due to dementia but she has never accepted her own diagnosis.

Soon after, it became obvious to the family that Dad would not be able to keep looking after Mum, though he believed that was his role, his identity even. His cognitive ability was declining, his capacity to recognise and respond to Mum's needs becoming dangerously inadequate. They enabled each other to continue a semblance of independence while I fielded calls from the agency providing at-home carers, who were sounding alarms.

I was intensely distressed at having to force Mum to leave her home. She had grown up moving house and school almost yearly. This home was the haven she had craved for her first thirty years. They had designed it, built it and made a garden of a grassy wilderness, now filled with enormous trees and shrubs. She was adamant she would only leave in death. But it could not be that way. How could I leave her to die slowly of neglect in order to fulfil her wish? Yet I feared I would break the bond of trust we had if I made her move into residential aged care.

I prayed for God's mercy for my parents, who did not have the faith to pray for it themselves. God strengthened me with a promise that he would provide a way of mercy for us all through this seeming impasse. I clung to that hope.

By this stage, whenever Mum had a fall and needed ambulance officers to get her off the floor, she was refusing their advice that she go to hospital. One day I received a call saying she had fallen and that her heartbeat was very slow. I gave the approval for her hospital transfer. She was given a pacemaker, but the staff quickly realised that there were more complex issues. Three weeks later they reluctantly sent her home on the proviso that she should receive rehabilitation care there. Mum was not motivated to exercise at home. A month later she was back in hospital, again because I had intervened. This time the doctors diagnosed dementia and forbade her to return home. The combination of dementia, her physical condition, and Dad's cognitive capacity triggered the decision.

I wrote a poem about it.

I had been checking out aged care in our area for a while by then, and had chosen a home I felt she and Dad could be comfortable in. I had already given Mum's details to this facility, so when the doctors made their decision, I rang the home. Amazingly, there was a room available immediately. I took Dad to see it before signing the paperwork.

Grateful to have not had to force the issue alone, I visited her daily to demonstrate that I was not abandoning her. Mum adapted without complaint, particularly once we installed her favourite paintings. But it was difficult to know how she felt. That's part of her dementia, that she cannot express her emotions even though her language is intact.

Dad, in the meantime, was completely lost without Mum at home. My carer role shifted to supporting him, while all he wanted was to be with Mum. This did not, however, mean he was willing to move. That took another nine months, after his driver's licence was revoked and his mental health suffered, and mine with it. Once again, I was in the position of having to force a parent to move unwillingly. I couldn't do it, backing down the first time I tried. After some friends prayed at length with me, I had new courage to take the lead. It's a strange and uncomfortable responsibility to be the decision-maker for your parents who have been independent longer than you have been alive.

Another challenge, another poem.

The time finally came when Dad and I both needed the decision to be made. This time he accepted it, more for my sake than his. He had some understanding that looking after him was stressful for me, and he had become used to me making other decisions and arrangements for him. He hated the idea of my life being impacted by his needs even more than he hated leaving behind his beloved home and his remaining independence. Once again, a room was immediately available, and he liked it. We even had time to decorate it with his favourite artworks and furniture over several days, making it easier for him to feel at home there before moving day arrived. I feared he would balk on the day, but he took himself there at 3am, and was given breakfast by staff when they found him in his armchair!

And there was another poem, this one with a touch of relieved humour.

By the grace of God, the move was just in time. Three weeks later Covid-19 struck and the aged care home locked down. Dad and Mum were together while we could only call or write. Their food, medications, personal and medical care, and their social needs, were being met far better than they had at home in recent years, let alone if they had been there during lockdown.

I cannot downplay the loss for the elderly to leave behind the places of their memories and independence. Nobody wants to lose those. Taking responsibility for my parents' care, knowing they are no longer equipped to run their own lives, was possibly the hardest thing I have had to do. I am grateful that they still trust me, and that we have all seen God's mercy for us when so much was out of our control.

And, of course, there are the poems, so many poems, that have tracked the journey and helped me to lament and adapt.

One day my parents will die. I will grieve and feel the loss of their physical presence. I am confident I will see again all the mercies of God in the lives we have shared, even the lives we are living now.

And I will probably write a poem about it.

We Carry On
Esther Cremona

The day's mood swung between dazed astonishment and lip-pursing disbelief. Slightly perplexed trio. Mother, teenage daughter and pre-teen son.

A plethora of questions assaulted my brain in a harried train of thought. How am I going to home-school? Do I have enough chocolate? Are 30 books borrowed from the library sufficient? When did buying toilet paper become an Olympic sport in hoarding?

Shell-shocked at 9:48am precisely. I realised that a responsible adult needed to get this house organised. I gasped at the comprehension that the sensible person would be me.

'Self-isolation' was the phrase that I wrestled with on a regular basis. FaceTime, Zoom and Microsoft Teams drove me along a windy new learning curve. Learning to 'mute' oneself when coughing, sneezing or indeed encouraging children to please be quiet is a newly appreciated skill set.

Home-schooling, remote learning or learning online? Whichever moniker suited us for the learning at home concept didn't really matter. The boat we were in could be called anything, as each day the waves of learning could roll and toss us about in any direction.

The concept of living out an Enid Blyton style home-schooling scenario was crudely shattered. Not a gleeful skip in sight. No 'hurrah for Mother' was forthcoming. I had visions of waking up peacefully sleeping children. Warm pyjama cuddles and early morning breakfasts together. Proudly displaying their completed school work each afternoon. Apparently, in the crushing reality of confounding times this is not a realistic vision.

I would have very much welcomed a Magic Faraway Tree.

'Can I keep my pj's on today?'

'My iPad isn't charged.'

'I'm hungry. But I don't want to eat *that*.'

'Can I shop online for new clothes?'

'MUM! Do you have to sing out loud? It hurts me.'

'When can I see my friends again?'

God help me.

I answered each question calmly, in my best Mary Poppins voice. A slightly strained, less than lilting, gravelly sounding Mary Poppins at best. Home-school, they said. It will be fun, they said.

Trying for some semblance of isolation sanity, I had prepared a folder of handy home-schooling hints. These may, or may not have been followed, or perhaps they collected a little dust along the way. To remember who would truly sustain us during challenging times, a printed copy of Psalm 91 sat at the very front of the folder. Pandemic aside, Psalm 91 bought a welcome calm, when the world outside was a little disordered. We carried on.

By Day 20 of self-isolation and feeling mildly cracked, I ditched the school routine for a day and let my teenage daughter and pre-teen son teach me how to play 'Sonic Racing', a game on their X-box. We laughed, relaxed and forgot about the mild Armageddon in the world for a short while. Although, according to my homebound critics, I play X-box like a 'demented chicken'.

'Driveway-chats' and 'lawn socials' entered into our world at home. Maintaining our distance but needing some face-to-face human interaction was invaluable. Scene set-ups involving strategically placed camp chairs, alongside packets of disinfectant wipes, bottles of hand sanitiser and cans of Glenn-20 became the norm. Nothing romantic about sliding a cup of tea to a loved friend with a sturdy length of cardboard, yet it was a whole new way of connection. Gloved hand throwing a Tim-Tam across the open garage door shows dedication to care on new levels of friendship. But discovering Tim-Tams in individually wrapped packets that don't run the risk of being ruined by hitting the cement floor really was marvellous.

Sunny days paved the way for outside walks. I thought playing a song called 'Sunshine Day' by the very entertaining Brady Bunch would get the children just as excited as I was to frolic outdoors. It did not. Yet it didn't stop my occasional descent into 70s and 80s childhood memorabilia. I called it 'emotional self-regulation'. My children called it 'getting old'.

Once the original shock of self-isolation at home subsided, there really were roller-coaster days of emotions, thoughts and angst. Beach walks became a regular activity to smooth out a myriad of bumpy moods. Inhaling fresh air, and watching fluffy white clouds roll unhurried across an azure blue sky. Waves that caressed the shoreline, whispering a soft hush. Enjoying and stretching out the simplicity of meandering the coastline, until my brood would ask how much farther would I make them go? A new feeling of mentally calculating the distance on how far others were walking near us and were there too many people around?

We Carry On

Checking dates and days as they began to meld together. Feeling great some days and the reality of some gloomy thoughts on other days became familiar. At one point, my boat became a little wobbly as I tried in vain to hold on by myself during the storm. Truthfully feeling overwhelmed and somewhat alone I needed to cast a line. A line of anxiety to the one I knew would be willing to take on all of my burden.

On Day 32 I sat in my walk-in wardrobe. Just to breathe and get my heart and head right with God. After all being together every day for some weeks now, it wasn't long before two sets of footsteps crept quietly outside the door. Loudly whispered, a question reaches me.

'Mum, what are you doing in there?'

'Narnia business.'

Well, I thought it was funny.

Can anyone who has read CS Lewis honestly say they've never given the world-beyond-a-wardrobe a try?

Forty-two days in total we three champions spent under one roof. Twenty-four hours, seven days per week. Without any helpful manuals, aptly titled *Pandemic Parenting: A guide for Dummies.* Yet, we made it.

Some of my time was spent blogging, for the first thirty or so days in self-isolation. A light-hearted whimsy daily-diary of sorts, aiming to bring a few moments of distraction, a smile or perhaps a laugh out loud.

We had challenges, moments of fear, a couple of tears and remained grateful for every blessing.

Although, one big question remains.

Did we have enough library books? Yes! Yes, we did.

The Wise Old Owl
Val Russell

Woah! What a stunning creature. Perfect feathers with intense colourings, shades of browns and yellows and jet-black eyes that stared down at me. He was so close. I blinked a few times in case I was dreaming, but the owl was very real. Turning his head to the left he looked up the driveway and I continued walking inside...

With our very large, bright red suitcases packed to bulging, neatly stacked near the front door, the tension and anxiety in the air was as thick as the Lyles golden syrup sitting on the kitchen table. It felt sticky and tangible. Everywhere I looked the uncomfortable atmosphere stuck to me, like label adhesive, stubbornly determined to be left behind after the label is removed. Tomorrow we would be leaving Australia to work overseas for two years, while two of our three children stayed behind. How did I ever conclude this was a good thing to do? Only a crazed mother would leave her teenagers to fend for themselves for the next two years. A decision made from some type of numbness that is difficult to explain was now, the night before leaving, becoming a reality I was unsure I could face.

The pressure cooker was rising. Any minute the top would pop off, a moment I always dreaded as a child. In this case, though, steam was not going to burn me. The emotional trauma of making such a life changing decision for our family caused my heart to burn up. Pressure pressed in from all sides with my husband desperate to go, two of my girls assuring me they would be fine and could look after themselves and the screams from within that said mothers don't leave their girls during these important, impacting years. The tear ripped from the bottom of my heart to the top as I

The Wise Old Owl

agonised over the decision I needed to make. The pain became excruciating and stayed that way even after I gave in to the pressure, deciding that we should go. It never really went away, just settled itself somewhere deep in my heart so I could get through the impossible moments that were to follow. For my autistic way of thinking and seeing, changing circumstances and an unknown future were more than unbearable to consider, causing the anxiety of the situation to build up to an incredible level and leaving me no option but to 'check out' from my present world. I relied on others to tell me what to do, going through the motions of being a mother, albeit a very 'absent' mother.

Although desperate for my children to know how I felt, I was unable to express my thoughts and feelings. I could not see past the fear that froze me in my tracks. I coped the only way I knew how. Putting one foot in front of the other, I robot-walked my way through that day and many to follow with an emotionally blank existence. Well, mostly. There were times when unwanted emotions escaped to horrify me and confirm how vulnerable I really was. Every conscious moment I cried out to God for confirmation or explanation about how this traumatic experience could possibly be his will.

'Did you see that owl, Mum?' Jen, our eighteen year old, in the middle of her first year at university, asked at the dinner table. Shocked by the sound of her voice in an otherwise quiet room, I was jolted back to reality.

'I did. Very beautiful. In all our ten years of living in this place I have never seen an owl here before,' I replied in my monotone voice. As a child I had been very interested in birds and my thoughts drifted to the barn owls of England. Beautiful birds with what appeared to be perfectly round eyes and an amazing display of intricately designed feathers. Their ability to turn their heads two hundred and seventy degrees fascinated me. As a child I was convinced they turned their head a full circle. To me owls are stunningly handsome, intelligent creatures and as a young person I aspired to be similar. Quiet, smart and ready to survive in an ever-changing world. Memories.

'Probably just a boobook owl or something.' Liz ate her meal quietly, her strong ambivalent feelings silently consuming her thoughts.

'Nah. It's special. I know it is.' Bella, the youngest at thirteen, was confident and often able to sense spiritual connections to certain things.

'Yeah, it's special' agreed Jen, 'I'm going to take a photo in the morning.'

Dinner continued with the click clacking of cutlery and the continuous flow of safety instructions my husband was outlining for Jen and Liz to follow while we were away. As their father, he was determined to make sure the girls were safe and secure facing such a new level of independence. What I had not considered was the volatile nature of their relationship with each other. They would be staying in our house, caring for themselves, along with our totally annoying, hyperactive dog.

It had been a rough day and I longed for bed but going to bed would bring the morning and the dreadful goodbyes that awaited us at the airport. Finally, after weighing then re-arranging and re-weighing bags, to make sure we had what we thought we would need and still stay within weight, it was time for bed. A massive sadness welled up inside me about leaving my precious girls behind. I would not be saying goodnight to them tomorrow night or the one after, in fact I didn't know when I would be able to say goodnight to them again, or make them a hot chocolate, or a birthday cake. 'STOP,' my head screamed. I needed to quit processing all this or I would go completely insane. I had taught the girls all they needed to know to look after themselves, but they were my flesh and blood and all the experiences in the world would never make up for being separated from my awesome girls. I pondered whether this was truly God's plan. How could something so painful be God's plan?

I never heard the owl hoot at all. A bit like God, I guess. Often, I never hear God speak specifically or 'clearly' enough for me to be truly convinced about something, but maybe he likes to beat around the bush by sending symbols and hidden messages. Maybe sending the owl was his way of saying 'I am with you and your girls forever'. Hindsight is a wonderful thing. Even though in those very challenging moments the owl's presence was a fascinating experience, I realise now that its presence was full of purpose and promise. I read once that owls are a symbol of paranormal wisdom, regal silence and fierce intelligence. I am inclined to agree. The owl in our tree was a tangible presence of something unseen, greater than any living being, that left us feeling in awe of the Creator, who had taken a moment to comfort us, with the presence of a 'wise old owl'.

As I dragged my case up the steps to the car, I looked one last time at the owl sitting on a branch just above the trunk of the large tree shading our front porch. Many a possum had inhabited the tree and powerlines nearby, but never an owl. I wanted to stop and say hello, touch it to make sure it was real, but I dared not disturb this beautiful creature. I was later to learn that, when the very emotional girls returned home from the airport later that morning, the owl still sat quietly observant in the tree. He remained there for a whole week and to my knowledge has never since returned. I believe the beautiful bird was a symbol reminding us that God was, and continues to be, perfectly wise, incredibly supernatural, infinitely intelligent and in control of our future.

Mum, Meet My Mother
Jo Wanmer

It felt weird. We were driving our daughter to meet her mother. For eighteen years I had been her mother, her only mother. However, we had always explained that she had come out of another woman's tummy. As a three year old she had stamped her feet, declaring, 'I didn't want to be in another lady's tummy!'

The opinionated three year had morphed into a beautiful, independent, and yes, opinionated young woman. All these years, we had talked about her birth mother, wondered who she was and what she was like. She'd often wondered if she even remembered. I had promised to help locate her once she turned eighteen. But our efforts were unnecessary as her birth mother had rung me on the day of her birthday. It was a bittersweet contact. We didn't have to search, but I had to face the reality of another mother, whose love was shown by her reaching out. Now the day was here. We were on our way to meet this mythical person.

The route was familiar. The two-hour journey took forever, so it seemed. What would she be like? Look like? We had spoken to her on the phone and had ascertained she shared our daughter's skinny legs and ample breasts. She was very keen to see her, had organised a meeting as soon as possible. Spontaneous – just like our daughter, her daughter.

But would she be welcoming? Easy to talk to? We continued to drive despite our daughter's random demands to turn around. Ten minutes later she'd be excited again. Then desperate. As I said, it was a very long two hours.

As her mother, it was a strange sensation. Raising teenagers is never easy but the last few years with our daughter was filled with unique challenges. Had I mothered well enough? Would she connect with this woman in such a way that she didn't need me anymore? I'd cared for her, nursed her, fought for her in all sorts of spheres. She, more than anyone, had taught me about love, the gritty, messy, unconditional love. Our relationship had been through severe fires of testing and our love was now strong. But today changed everything. What does one say to the woman who gave up her baby? What would she think of us? She had already babbled over the phone, excited that her daughter's parents were still together, that she was in a stable home.

Her father and I waited in the car whilst our girl gulped a deep breath and knocked on the door. Within minutes, an auntie came from the house and, with a warm smile, invited us to join them. Inside, it was hard to know who was talking the most, but they paused as we were introduced.

'Mum, Dad, meet my mother.'

These two women, birth mother and daughter, instinctively related to each other, both talking at once. They shared a common taste in dress, even owning some of the same clothes. Their hair was dyed the same colour and they smoked similar cigarettes. They were both the only ones in their families who smoked.

I sat and watched them, amazed. Our daughter's tastes had always been very different to ours – but now it seemed they were the same as her birth mother's. Intrigued, and a little alarmed, I watched for other genetic connections.

As I chatted with the aunt, I told her our daughter had named her pet budgerigar 'Shovel'. We laughed together about the crazy name.

Her new mother's ears picked up the story. 'Why did you choose that name?'

My daughter grinned. 'It is the model of Harley Davidson I hope to own one day.'

Her birth mother stood, an unreadable expression on her face. 'Come with me.'

Mystified, we followed her through the house to the garage. She pointed to an object covered by a tarp. 'Have a look.'

With a bemused glance at me, our daughter lifted the cover and screamed. A Harley Davidson Shovel motor bike gleamed in their garage. Her dream bike was owned by our daughter's birth father.

Then I understood. So many facets of my daughter's character, that we struggled to understand, became clear. Her genes were stronger than many of the things we tried to teach her. I was so glad I'd released my control on her clothing choices. Her smoking made sense. Although our family modelled no smoking and she agreed with her mind, in her body there was a greater pull.

So was our training, guiding and discipline a total waste of time? Had we spent all those years trying to put a square stick in a round hole? What would she do now she had found her 'missing pieces'? Her birth father wasn't there that day as he was working in the mines. But they were living together. Both her parents. She had the fairy tale ending.

Later that afternoon as we drove home, she filled the car with stories and excitement. There were already arrangements for them to get together again. This return trip was a quick two hours.

A big question loomed in my mind. 'Is there room for us in this new story?' I squirrelled the question away, asking God for grace and wisdom. We were Christian conservatives. The other couple worldly. Many of our guidelines would seem unnecessary to them. Yes, the lady was lovely, and thanked us over and over for raising her so well. There was no indication that she wanted to take over now. But would our daughter gravitate that way?

All we could do, as her parents, was to commit her to the Lord and his keeping. Once again, we laid down our claim to her and trusted the Lord to watch over her and keep her. Yes, there were tears, as there always are when we surrender another part of our life to him.

A few days later, I lounged in a double beanbag before our open fire, watching the flames, relaxing. This precious daughter came in and joined me on the bean bag. We just snuggled for a while in silence. She pushed up on one elbow and looked at me. 'She's lovely, my birth mother, but she's still a stranger. She's not my Mum. You will always be my mum.'

Now, twenty-five years later, our family is still close. Yes, another family enriches the mix, but this adult daughter is still my girl.

Rescued
Susan Brown

'Do you think we should go to the hospital?' My husband's words broke through the haze clouding my mind.

I dragged my head up and sighed. For hours I'd been lying on the bedroom floor, mostly face down, trying to find a position where my body didn't hurt so much. It had taken all my strength to push myself high enough to vomit into a bowl. Mark had woken and climbed out of bed to come to my side.

I had hoped this sickness – whatever it was – would have settled through the night. Surely, after almost two days, I should have been improving. Instead, the nausea of Sunday afternoon had developed into violent retching, shaking fevers, diarrhoea and overwhelming weakness. Tightness under my ribcage made breathing difficult and my head spun.

Mark had already suggested I go to hospital – several times. Each time, I'd refused. The thought of spending hours vomiting in a waiting room full of people was unbearable. This time he was determined. 'I think we should pray about it.'

'What time is it?' I breathed.

'Four o'clock.'

'Okay. I'll try.'

We spent a few minutes praying quietly. At that moment, my mum woke in her Sydney home, burdened to pray – she already knew I was very unwell.

'So, what did you think?'

With eyes closed, I mumbled, 'I keep getting the word "appendix".' The sharp pain in my lower abdomen was constant. 'Maybe we should just go and get it checked.'

'Okay.' He stood, slipped his hands under my arms and helped me to my feet. Every movement was agony. Mark woke our oldest son, telling him we were leaving, and we shuffled together out to the car, our breath forming steamy clouds in the icy night air.

At the hospital, I slumped over my sick bowl, my head resting on my arms. The room was quiet, almost empty. A random thought ambled through my mind, *Am I just being a drama queen?*

'Hello, Susan.' A calm voice spoke close to my face. 'Your husband explained what's been happening. Can you sit up so I can take a few vitals?'

I pushed myself off the bowl, willing my rolling eyes to meet hers. 'I know you,' I slurred.

Recognition sounded in her voice. 'Oh, yes. I think we'll take you straight in.' She strode away, returning moments later with a wheelchair.

'Sorry,' I breathed. 'I can't remember your name.'

'Don't worry about that,' she answered briskly. 'Let's just see if we can make you better.' She wheeled me through double doors into a curtained cubicle then returned to the admissions desk.

Two nurses changed me into a thin hospital gown, applied a heart monitor and provided anti-nausea medication. A short time later, they wheeled my bed to a larger space at one end of the department, 'so we can get more people around you.' Four more nurses swelled their numbers and a doctor came periodically. They gave me an oxygen mask, injected morphine, took blood, inserted a catheter and introduced a drip to each forearm. The doctor threaded a long picc line (peripherally inserted central catheter) through a vein in my neck, attaching its multi-stranded end to five IV bags. Warm, soft blankets—so many blankets—were draped one atop another over my shivering body.

I sensed the pain, the darkness, extending upwards and turned to the nurse closest to me, patting my ribcage. 'It's moving into my chest.' She exchanged glances with a colleague. I couldn't read their expressions.

Soon after, a doctor appeared beside me. 'Susan, it seems you have an infection, but your pathology results won't be ready for a while. We've started you on five different antibiotics to make sure we hit whatever bacteria is at work. Once we get the test results back, we'll narrow them down to the right one. We're also giving you IV fluids to help lift your blood pressure.'

'Okay.' I understood. I'd glanced at the monitor a few times. My blood pressure had dropped by almost half.

I heard my husband's concerned voice respond. 'Do you *have* to use so many antibiotics? She's just come off a course of them and they've left her very run-down.'

Instantly a nurse's voice snapped from the other side of the room, 'Your wife is in a state of *septic shock*. If we don't give her antibiotics she'll *die*.'

I could barely make sense of her words. *Die? Really? I'm in hospital – surely that means I'm safe.* I lifted a faint prayer, *Lord, I'm in your hands.*

Hours ticked by. Antibiotics and fluids flowed steadily. Staff hovered, watching my vital signs. My catheter bag remained empty, implying my kidneys had failed. Many times, they asked me,

'What's your full name? When were you born? Where do you live?'

Mark's presence beside me was calm and constant. He sent out a message, asking for prayer, reaching hundreds of people across the nation and beyond. Several friends, on reading the message, sensed the intensity of my battle and immediately began fighting for me in prayer.

Six hours passed. Still no change. Doctors came in and out, teams of interns tailing them. During one visit, a senior doctor told Mark, 'It's good you came in when you did. If you'd left it even one hour longer, it may have been too late.'

Finally, the medical staff opted to give me a very high dose of noradrenalin. Gradually my blood pressure rose to a safer level. I was taken for a CT scan then a laparoscopy, where they drained a large volume of fluid from my abdomen. The surgeon found my appendix was inflamed, but didn't need removing.

It was a few days before we learned the nurse's words were true. I had sepsis, a severe response to infection which inflames the whole body, damaging multiple organs. In one out of three cases – like mine – the cause is unknown. Septic shock, the most extreme form of sepsis, kills one out of every two victims.

I spent the following week in Intensive Care. Collapsed lungs and pneumonia added to my list of challenges, dampening my recovery. After two days of forced bed-rest, clear fluids and continued oxygen I was allowed to try walking with a frame. A few days later I managed on my own. The residual fluid in my system pooled in my legs and stomach, swelling them so much my skin hurt. I wore long pressure stockings and shuffled around the ward, trying to bring improvement. All my muscles were so sore and weak, even the simplest of actions left me exhausted.

When I returned home, our family of six were flooded with support. Mum flew down from Sydney, followed by one of my sisters. They ably kept our household running, releasing me to rest. Our friends were loving and generous, keeping us in prayer and providing delicious meals for the next month.

It felt strange to be so frail, so dependent and limited in what I could do. Every little milestone was cause for celebration – sleeping on my side instead of propped up on my back, walking to the mailbox, squatting to get something out of the cupboard. It was three months before I could manage without an afternoon sleep, nine months before I felt normal again.

Several doctors had tried to tell me how severely ill I'd been, but it wasn't until my follow-up appointment a month after the illness that my eyes were opened. The surgeon ran through his medical checks and confirmed I was recovering well, then perched on the edge of his desk, dropped his professional tone and looked at me with gentle eyes. He said, 'I went home that night and said to my wife, "We had a mother of four in today and she nearly died."' I gaped, my eyes brimming with tears. I knew I *could have* died but didn't realise I'd come so very close.

In July this year I celebrated eight years of 'bonus life'. I realise there were so many 'ifs' in my experience, the outcome could have been very different:

If we hadn't gone to hospital…

If emergency had been busy and there were fewer staff available to help…

If the medics had taken longer to make a diagnosis…

If people hadn't bothered to pray when they heard I was sick…

God reigns over the 'ifs'. He knows all the days he has planned for me and, in his kindness, he put everything in place that cold July morning to ensure they were not cut short.

The words in Psalm 31:14-15, 'My times are in your hands,' are a tangible reality to me now, a source of clarity and focus. Every day is a gift to be embraced and lived to the full. God created me for a purpose. My greatest desire is to discover and fulfil it.

A Mended Heart
Jenny Woolsey

One wooden cross.
Two anxious parents.
Three holes in a tiny heart.

Standing at the door of the operating theatre, my seven-month-old in my arms, I looked at the theatre nurse in her blue scrubs. It was time.

'Are you ready?' she asked me after Jessica's medical records had been handed to her by our escort.

I nodded as peace pulsed through my veins. I kissed Jessica on her mop of light brown hair and surrendered her to the arms of the nurse. I then turned around and did not look back.

The wait was long…Seconds turned into minutes turned into hours. But as the clock ticked, prayers of protection and for the success of the surgery were being offered to God from all corners of the globe.

Jessica, my youngest of three, was born with Down syndrome. This diagnosis was a shock when it came at four weeks of age, but we accepted it and saw it as God's will for her and for us. Half of all babies born with Down syndrome have a congenital heart defect, so it was mandatory that she undergo an echocardiogram.

The cardiologist had placed his stethoscope on Jessica's chest and, after listening for a minute, said, 'Her heart sounds fine. There shouldn't be any problems but we will have a check just to make sure.'

His sharp, 'Oh', as the transducer pressed against her chest and he stared at the image on the screen, sent a chill up and down my spine. I tried to interpret the blue and red flashing lights but I couldn't.

Things were actually *not* okay.

Jessica had three holes in her heart – in medical terms, an AVSD PDA. The defects would require open heart surgery. The 'miracle', as the cardiologist called it, was that her heart had the perfect pressure in it to stop the blood from mixing. And that was why her heart sounded okay on his initial examination.

Each proceeding month we took our baby back to have an echocardiogram. At each of these appointments we were told, 'She will have her surgery within a month.'

But…the month would pass on by.

Anxiety began to smoulder.

Around five months of age we noticed Jessica's lips were turning blue, she was struggling to feed and she was sleeping more. Her heart was deteriorating.

More prayers went up to heaven and we had her baptised at church.

That month passed on by.

Anxiety became a campfire.

Finally, at seven months, a hospital-logo printed envelope arrived. I opened it with shaky fingers. The surgery date for a fortnight's time was written in black and white.

The anxiety became a wildfire. Questions swirled such as what if something went wrong or if she died? We had nearly lost our eldest to a bleed during one of her skull surgeries – and now here we were – we could lose our baby.

Admission day arrived. We dressed Jessica in a new pretty floral dress that had been sent from her grandmother in America.

A Mended Heart

Jessica was lying in the cot when the surgeon knocked on the door and entered.

'I have just read her notes and I need to do an echocardiogram to see if she needs the surgery now,' he stated.

My eyes popped open like wild-west wagon wheels and I suddenly felt sick. He was implying that she may not have the surgery even though we had been admitted!

As the transducer marched over Jessica's chest, I worried. Red and blue flashes on the screen showed the direction of the blood.

There was silence in the room. Even Jessica was mute.

The doctor turned the machine off, wiped Jessica's chest with a cloth to get rid of the excess gel, then turned to face me.

What would he say? My gut was queasy. What if we had to go home?

'We will go ahead with the surgery tomorrow morning...'

Nine words. Nine words that calmed me for that moment.

I sighed in my head and dressed Jessica.

The next morning, our close friends arrived. Kay gave Jessica a small handcrafted wooden cross to hold. This became a pacifier as it was instantly sucked on. We all prayed.

The nurse appeared. 'It's time,' she said.

I carried Jessica in my arms as we weaved through the 'staff only' doors and corridors to the nurse waiting in her blue scrubs. Deep in my heart I knew that Jessica was in God's hands and the outcome would be what he wanted it to be.

Eventually, my mobile phone rang and we were told by a nurse that Jessica was out of surgery and to proceed to PICU. I thanked God that she had survived.

Adults lay in stark white beds as we made our way to the far corner. In a bed, our tiny delicate baby lay attached to a ventilator, a monitor displaying her stats and hooked to a multitude of tubes and drains. Down her sternum, a long red scar brought tears to my eyes.

There was no recliner beside the bed, which I was used to from my other children's surgeries, and I asked the nurse if I could stay somewhere at the hospital. Her response was that I lived too close and they were reserved for out-of-town parents. I would have to go home and come back the next day. If I could drive, it would not have been an issue but, as I have low vision and I cannot drive, it was an issue.

I rang my friends who had gone home by that stage and asked for prayer – for God to intervene and work another miracle.

The social worker came to see me and I explained my situation. She agreed that I needed to stay.

That first night, lying on the hard mattress in a strange smelling tiny room, the pent up emotions of the day swept through me. Tears flowed down my cheeks and I earnestly prayed. I thanked God and praised him for bringing Jessica safely through the surgery and I asked for her protection and healing through the night.

The next morning, after a fitful sleep, I arose early and made my way back to see my baby. At her bedside, I immediately asked the nurse how she was.

'She's good,' was her reply.

I let out a huge lungful of air and sat down on the adjacent chair, reaching out to take Jessica's small hand in mine.

The surgeon came by on his rounds.

A Mended Heart

'It was good they didn't give her the extra bag of fluids,' he said. 'She has a partially collapsed lung but that is normal. She's doing really well.'

When I questioned the nurse what he meant, she told me that usually there is a set amount of fluid that the baby is given. It was decided during the night to only give her half. If Jessica had been given the full amount, she would have become swollen and have needed to be drained – a serious complication was avoided.

I thought about this a lot. I didn't believe in coincidences or things just happening. I believed that God stopped the extra fluids from being given to her.

Jessica was quickly moved out of PICU and into a high dependency ward. Daily global prayers continued to cover her. She soon went into a private room.

When Jessica was asleep, I would wander the cardiac ward reading story plaques which accompanied large black and white portraits of smiling children. Many of these were memorials. My heart broke for those parents.

Two weeks later, we packed our bags to go home. Regular echocardiograms would keep an eye on the functioning of her heart. We hoped Jessica wouldn't need any more heart surgeries but, if she did, we knew that God would again be in control.

One wooden cross.

Two thankful parents.

Three repaired holes in a tiny heart.

Green Velvet
Joy Leabrooke

I've always been a colours person. They speak to me.

I remember my childhood bedroom. I'd swing between themes of pale blue and a dusky pink, raiding my mother's linen closet for any fabrics and bedding I could use, because colours *had* to match. We were poor I later found out – a fact that eventually explained why my primary school friend had a chandelier and I did not – but it was not a fact that bothered me at that time because I was too busy creating beauty in my bedroom world and celebrating the beauty God was creating in his world outside.

I would get up early to photograph the lemon gold sunrise through the powerlines from our concrete porch. When the morning glory vine shut its purple wafer flowers tight, I would climb onto our shed roof to capture the apricot and lilac sunset light poised above our back fence. I barely remember hearing the noises of the factory that clanged behind that fence, because the colours, they spoke to me so clearly. Beyond that factory was a busy road, but I felt I lived in the countryside, in Eden. Sitting on the bus waiting for our stop, I always knew I was home when the roadside houses changed into tall blue-green gums swaying against an impossibly blue sky.

I remember wondering why it was said, 'Blue and green should never be seen', when it was obviously God's favourite colour combination, followed by pink and red sunset skies and blue and bleached sandy beaches. Poor 'Anne with an e' who never got to wear pink just because she had red hair! I had red-toned hair and thought pink looked beautiful on me when paired with brown. It went with my eyes. Any colour combination good enough for God was good enough for me – he knew his palette and I spent my childhood memorising it.

All those colours, they thrilled my eyes and spoke to my heart. Blue was the colour of God's love for us all, as vast and eternal as the sea and the sky. Beach trips meant wandering for hours on the shore, marvelling at how God could throw our sins into the deepest sea and remember them no more. Apricot was the colour of God's personal love for me, discovered in encounters with fragrant roses the colour of my skin as I went roaming with God through our neighbourhood. The perfect blooms showed me how God saw me; the imperfect ones reassured my perfectionist self that despite my faults I couldn't help but be beautiful – it was how I was made.

If I had to choose a favourite colour, however, it would be green. It speaks of renewal and growth and so much more. Green is the colour of God's intimate understanding of me, and the way he soothes my soul by meeting my little yet oh-so important needs.

When I got married at twenty-two I was thrilled to have a whole house to decorate. Intense orange and yellow net curtains teamed with a scratchy brown couch and yellow and brown parquetry-patterned carpet had tortured my aesthetics my whole childhood. But the truth was, my young husband and I didn't have a great deal more money than we'd had in childhood, and there came a time when not even my most economic efforts at home decorating were possible. My husband was out of a job and we had two small girls in a modest private school.

We moved back into my old family home, renting from my parents working overseas. By then, the loathed orange net curtains had been replaced by inoffensive white net, but the yellow net curtains remained in the rumpus with the parquetry carpet. And in the bedroom my husband and I now occupied were my mother's pride and joy, the first pretty pair of floral curtains she'd ever been able to buy. They clashed with everything I owned.

I asked my husband if I could buy some calico fabric to sew plain curtains to replace them, but he said no, we really didn't have the money. I didn't push him, knowing school fees and food really were more important, despite my dismay. But in my heart I prayed, 'Lord, please, I need some curtains for the bedroom – simple off-white I think would do, but if you have something else in mind, I'll take it, because you know best. The only thing is it needs to be free.'

I'm not sure how I expected God to answer that prayer, but this is how he did...

Down the street lived a family friend who went to my childhood church, a kind old lady from Malta who had helped my parents teach me about God when I was very young. So now I was back in the neighbourhood I went to visit her. With warmth she drew me into her home, asking before I could even begin a conversation, 'Would you happen to need some curtains? I am in the middle of getting some replaced.' Yes, it was that simple – free curtains. But would they actually be any better than what I had? They had to match.

Well, they weren't off-white – green velvet, that's what they were. The perfect size, and as it turned out, the perfect colour. I hung them up in the bedroom and through the windows I watched

Green Velvet

the silver birch's shimmering green and knew deep in my heart that God saw me and understood me. My free curtains were the perfect verdant frame to my peaceful view, but even more importantly, they were the same colour and texture as my second-hand lounge set and dining chairs – velvet green. The God who made the entire universe cared about my colours matching! He knew how I was made. He knew what I would love even when I couldn't imagine it. I was not an obsessive perfectionist who needed to learn to put up with perfectly good curtains, I was *loved*.

So I prayed again, and a friend from church offered me a pile of white net curtains she no longer used. It is the only time in my life I have ever been offered 6 metres of curtains and it was just enough to replace those yellow net curtains in the rumpus!

And as the years have gone by, green velvet has continued to speak of how I have been fearfully and wonderfully made, how deeply God cares about little me. When the original three-seater couch needed to be replaced, we still didn't have any money to spend, but I had sixty dollars of birthday money. So, I put my faith in the car and went op-shopping with the Lord. 'I need a new couch, Lord, and it has to be no more than sixty dollars.' The first op-shop I went to had a three-seater couch. In green velvet. For sixty dollars. When the single chairs from that old lounge set needed replacing, we collected the club sofas my husband had loaned to his sister when we got married. Green velvet again. Those green velvet curtains followed us from house to house, my reminder of God's faithfulness toward the desires of my heart until they went mouldy in our draughty Canberra house.

Now, fifteen years later, back in my hometown, I sit on my green velvet dining chair at my kitchen table writing this story, having dreamed it into being in one of my green velvet club sofas in our little family room. Those chairs have long been in need of respringing, but in the absence of the money to do so, I picked up two green velvet European pillows in a Spotlight sale bin and now they're perfectly comfortable again.

In fact, it's the best seat in the house, my green velvet club sofa – my prayer chair. When I sit there, stroking the velvet of the arms, I am reminded that I am right in the middle of God's provision and care. His face shines toward me, he delights in who I am and in my delight in him. And he cares about matching colours, because he cares about me.

The Unexpected Calling
Baxter Gierus-Heintze

I was in Adelaide.

Not alone, of course. It was 2019, and I wasn't even fourteen yet. Dad was driving, and Papa was front seat.

It was a welcome getaway. There was just too much going on at school. Too much work. Too much stress.

We turned down a thin alley. Then another. And another.

Finally, we parked. At the Titanium Security Arena, a basketball stadium.

This, ladies and gentlemen, was a once in a lifetime opportunity. No, we weren't seeing the basketball.

We were going to see Franklin Graham, son of legendary preacher Billy Graham.

The line was already ten metres back, and we still had to wait for almost two hours. Papa decided to sit down, so Dad and I kept standing. The sun's rays beat down on us, and we were sweating like dogs.

Finally, the doors opened. By that time, we were near the front of the line, and the line was back at least two kilometres.

First there were the bands. Planetshakers were up first, a Christian pop band. Papa wasn't too fond of them because they were 'TOO LOUD,' he said, in his stiff German accent. Then there was David Crowder, a Christian country rock star who Dad and I liked.

One of Crowder's songs that was our favourite was 'I Saw The Light.' It's about someone who finally comes to God, which I thought was very fitting for that night.

Finally, up stepped Franklin Graham. He talked about how we always do the wrong things every day. But he also talked about forgiveness, through Jesus Christ. After some more talking, he invited people who hadn't received Christ yet to pray for his forgiveness.

What I saw next took my breath away.

For a good ten minutes, people slowly filed into the front. Just when I thought that was it, another hundred people made their way to the front. There must have been two thirds of the audience down at the front praying.

Then I felt the unexpected calling.

To be a pastor. It might seem strange for a thirteen year old, but since that night, I have never felt the need to be anything else. I felt that God was calling me, to serve in his church.

That, dear reader, wasn't the only unexpected calling that year. Far from it.

It was in the winter holidays, five months after I went to see Franklin Graham.

See, Mum is a teacher. On the first week of the winter school holidays, they stay at school and do special activities around Murray Bridge and surroundings.

One of those special activities was visiting the church at Coonalpyn. Where Dad was a pastor, and where we attended church.

Mum asked us to help out that day, so my sister Ella and I handed out small wooden crosses as the teachers filed into the church.

The Unexpected Calling

Now I don't know about you, dear reader, but meeting *all* the teachers at once outside of school, during the holidays; would you think that's awkward?

It was definitely awkward for me.

Then there was a service, with all the teachers. We sat in the back. That was awkward too.

After that we went to talk with the teachers, as it was morning tea.

There were a few of my favourite teachers there, and I talked to them for a while. But none I talked to longer than my current English teacher.

That's not what I had envisaged in my mind. I hadn't had her as my English teacher for long.

She said she would send me some information about a few competitions that she thought I would be interested in.

After a bit more talking, we walked home (it's right next to the church, so yeah, we walked).

Mum suggested I look at what my English teacher sent me.

Days passed.

I didn't look at it.

It got to the point where Mum literally demanded that I look at what my English teacher sent me (it was still during the holidays).

Reluctantly I did.

There were two competitions my English teacher told me about.

The first was a video competition, which, to be frank, was more boring than watching paint dry.

The second? It was perfect. It was a certain Christian writing competition.

I knew exactly what to write about.

I wrote furiously. I wrote about my Grandma and Gran, who went to heaven the previous year, and how much an impact that has had on me. Because, apart from Papa (and my parents), they were my main two mentors. They helped me navigate life's rough waters. They had an incredible faith, which, I wrote, is all that matters.

I titled it *The Happy Memoir* and sent it in on the first anniversary of my Grandma's passing.

I ended up in second place. I used the prize money to buy a keyboard. Whenever I play Elvis songs on my keyboard, I think of *The Happy Memoir* (Grandma liked Elvis).

But that's not the point.

Why I entered was to share my story of faith, how God has impacted my life. And not just my life; other lives as well. I want my stories to have an impact on other people's lives, including you, dear reader.

God had a reason for me to talk to the English teacher. To lead me to this.

For that, I am truly thankful.

Small Things
Shaoey C.

At the start of my school years, in 2015, I started reception. I was the shyest person you'd meet, and the most introverted little kid. I was lucky enough to have already known many kids there from my pre-school.

I still remember the first day of 'big' school as everyone called it, and constantly crossing my fingers, hoping my friends would be in my class. Creeping into class, with my Winnie the Pooh backpack – kids running around, laughing and giggling. I remember getting handed a Hello Kitty colouring sheet and getting my new pencil case out of my bag.

Over the first term, I was quite shy at lunch and recess, but I hung out with my group of friends. My best friends at the time – Sienna, Clementine, and Ruby – were the closest people I knew. Then I remember the day I met my soon-to-be-best-friend Chloe. It was nearing the end of day, and I was sitting around the playground while Chloe came up and started hanging around. I could already tell she was really energetic, the first time I saw her. We then started talking a bit and I met her best friend, Charlotte. I started hanging out with Charlotte and Chloe more often. Each new friend made was a small step for me.

Over the year my confidence started growing. I remember doing a simple spelling test, and getting promoted from the 'triangle' group to the 'square' group. I was very excited, as I was now with all my good friends at the time, Clem, Chloe and Charlotte. I still remember only getting 6/10, and not being able to get the word 'earthquake' correct two weeks in a row, but determined to as the rest of my friends got it correct. It seems childish now, but at that time it was the most important thing ever. It didn't change me as a person at all today, but at that time it was the thing that made me happy. It was pretty much the only thing I was focused on all week.

Even small things like being in a little trouble with the teacher were worrying for me. I thought about it at night, pleading that my teacher wouldn't remember and wouldn't hate me for it. I still remember the time I asked for help from the teacher, and she replied in an annoyed tone. It was a Wednesday, and I would only know if she was still upset on Monday when she was scheduled to teach us again.

On that Monday I apologised for asking, but she had no idea what I was talking about and said that whatever I did was fine. That's when I learnt that teachers don't hold a grudge on one tiny thing a student does, that it isn't their main priority.

Homework was a priority after school for me, and completely forgetting a task seemed like a disaster. One time, thinking I'd finished everything and already in bed, having said prayers and goodnight, I suddenly realised that I hadn't finished my English homework, due the next day. I shouted to my dad as he was leaving the room that I hadn't done it. I was so concerned about what the teacher would say, as I had heard when she chastised other students in my class.

I was nervous when walking into the classroom the next day, having all these thoughts about what she was going to say to me, and whether I would be in big trouble. I explained to my teacher that I didn't have my homework with me. She said what she normally would say, and just asked what I was going to write; I had to wing it and think of everything on the spot.

Small Things

Incidents like these were good to happen to me, as they made me learn small things that helped me. Tiny stuff like these seemed like the biggest problem in the world at the time, and the tension of this one thing that is overshadowing your mind for a while is stressful and scary. But after a week or so, none of it seems to have affected anything.

However, even though it seems like small things don't make a difference in life, it is really these little experiences added up that really do matter. Just like the background characters in a show; without them, the show wouldn't be as good.

The Rainbow
Jo-Anne Berthelsen

'She's going to ask you to take her funeral,' my friend's father tells me on the phone, his voice urgent. 'I wanted you to know before you visit her today.'

I am shocked, but manage to mumble a few words of thanks for forewarning me. Then I sit, staring into space, my mind whirling. How has it come to this? She is still young, with so much to live for. Why is she so determined not to eat? Yet I know, too, how strong a hold her illness has on her mind – and her body.

With dread in my heart I drive to see her and slowly climb the stairs to her apartment. She greets me in her usual warm, gentle way, but as I hug her, I feel the frailty and clamminess of her body. She is dying of her own choice. Yet, in another way, she is not free to choose. Those around her love her and want her to live, but her mind is like a steel trap that holds her captive and prevents her from responding in any normal, reasoned way.

We begin chatting, and I soon sense her desire to control everything that happens between us. I pray for God's wisdom and discernment. I know I need to be strong.

'I have something to ask you today,' she says at last, her voice calm and devoid of emotion. 'I'd like you to take my funeral. If you say yes, can we perhaps go through what I'd like to have in the service?'

I am silent for a few moments, then sense I have to meet her half way.

'Yes,' I tell her, the sadness almost overwhelming me. 'Yes, I will take your funeral when the time comes. But I don't want to discuss such things with you today. I want you to choose to live

The Rainbow

instead! You have so much to offer this world. God has great things for you to do yet.'

She is silent for some time. I can see my response has disappointed and even angered her, but I remain steadfast. She offers me a cup of tea and, as she makes it, I notice how she turns her back and quietly pours the nourishing energy drink she is supposed to have down the sink. I think of challenging her, yet feel helpless. I know she will give me a plausible explanation for her actions.

The weeks pass. Eventually, I hear she has sold her apartment and moved home to be with her parents some distance away. I keep in contact as best I can but, one Saturday when I phone, her father tells me the end is near. She has chosen to die at home and has refused any resuscitation efforts on her behalf.

Not long after, he contacts me to say she has passed away.

The following day, I drive to her parents' home, sad that they now have to explain to me what their daughter wanted for her funeral. Yet I know I could not have discussed this with her earlier. They are fragile, but we manage to arrange everything for the service in the church and then at the graveside.

A few days later I again drive to the town where they live, hoping I can get through what lies ahead. There are hundreds present at the church to support the grieving parents and honour the way they tried so hard to help their daughter. The hymns and Bible readings are beautiful and her mother shows such strength as she delivers a heartfelt eulogy. I speak, too, and hear the clear affirmation ripple across the congregation when I share some words of comfort and encouragement I believe are from God for the family: 'Well done! You did everything you could for her! I say it again because I think God wants you to know this deep in your hearts. Well done! You did *all* you could – and more.'

Afterwards, as refreshments are served, I wait until it is time for family and close friends to make the journey to the cemetery. I am last in the procession of cars heading back out to the highway and my mind reels as I try to keep up with the fast-moving hearse ahead. Time has slipped away and we are late, yet I drive carefully on the wet road, thankful the rain has now stopped. I am in unfamiliar territory in so many ways. I do not know where we are heading and have never taken a graveside service before. But I know God is with me and will see me through what lies ahead.

At last, we reach our destination and I follow the group of mourners up the green slope. As we gather together around the coffin, I am thankful for mutual friends nearby who smile at me in support.

I begin our little service in this beautiful, quiet place, the rolling hills stretching out behind us and the sky slowly clearing above. Everything goes well until it is time to commit my friend's body to the earth. I announce this will happen while we bow our heads in prayer and then I begin to pray. Yet when I finish, the coffin is still at ground level. Somehow, the men standing ready to undertake this task do not seem to have heard or understood my instructions.

For a moment, I wonder what to do next. Then, unbidden, an old chorus pops into my mind and a calmness comes over me. In a firm voice, I invite each person to take one of the beautiful roses cut especially for the occasion from the family's own garden and place it on the coffin as a final, loving, farewell gesture. One by one, they come – and I realise how much easier this is for everyone

The Rainbow

to do while the coffin is still at ground level, given the wet, slippery conditions.

Then I notice one of the undertakers approaching me.

'You're supposed to have told us to lower the coffin into the ground!' he whispers in an urgent tone.

'I thought I did that before I prayed,' I tell him. 'But don't worry! You can attend to it in a moment, while we all sing.'

He looks a little unconvinced, as he bows his head and moves off. Yet I know in my heart I have made the right choice. I gaze around at the little gathering, many of whom are now wiping away tears, after saying their final goodbyes in such a moving way.

'As our dear daughter, sister, aunt, niece and friend is lowered into the ground, let's join together in singing the old Scripture chorus 'Be still and know'. I will lead you, but I'd be grateful if some of you with strong voices would also help.'

I choose a key I hope is not too high and begin singing. Soon everyone joins in and, as our voices unite, a deep calmness descends on us all. We sing the chorus again, the same words over and over: *Be still and know that I am God. Be still and know that I am God. Be still and know that I am God.*

Yes, God is here, speaking to us all, I am sure.

The service is over and, one by one, we move off. I have done my best and now need to leave the family to be comforted by others. It is not until much later that I hear what happened for them on that hillside.

'As we sang that chorus,' my friend's father tells me eventually, 'a beautiful rainbow appeared above the hills behind you. It was such a special reminder to us that God is with us and is still in charge. Straight away, I knew in my heart this was God's unique way of reassuring us and comforting us.'

I had not seen that rainbow at all. I had been facing the opposite way, intent on leading our singing. God was at work, even when I was completely unaware.

Yet God had been there all along too. If I had not confused the undertaker with my instructions, we would not have sung that beautiful, old chorus. In fact, we would not have sung at all. And if we had not still been standing there, singing that simple song when the rainbow appeared, my friend's family may have missed out on seeing God's handiwork and sensing God's love for them in that moment.

Even in the darkest times, God cares.

Even when we do not know what to do, God cares.

Even when we do not see the rainbow, God cares.

Miracle Baby
Maggie Nerz Iribarne

At forty-three I'd accepted the idea of not having children and Jose, my husband, had already had a vasectomy when we'd met, so our baby was a stunner from the get-go. Having defied such odds, we were hopeful the repeat ultrasound would put an end to the doctor's suspicion that part of his brain was missing.

Instead she said, 'It's definitely not there.'

'Can it grow?' we asked.

'No. If it is not there now, it never will be.'

That bitter March day, my husband and I walked out to the parking lot silent, tearless. We went to Red Lobster and repeated short words and phrases to each other.

'What did she say? Maybe she's wrong?'

When we got home we started googling and that's when the panic set in. *Hydrocephaly, seizures, autism, blindness, profound learning disabilities, lifetime incontinence, inability to speak, inability to walk...*

The following week we went to see the priest. I sat in the rectory meeting room and sobbed to Father R, certain I was the cause of our son's disorder.

Father R stopped me mid-bawl. 'This. Is. Not. Your. Fault.'

Jose stood against the wall, speechless as Father R rubbed my hands with the oil for the sick and told me all my perceived sins were forgiven.

At 30 weeks, our son showed signs of early arrival and having lost all my amniotic fluid, I was hospitalised and put on extreme bed rest.

'Whose heart is that?' asked the doctors, checking the heart rate strips out at the main desk.

It was our son's, the strongest heart on the maternity floor.

The night before our son was born, a colleague sent out an email requesting that people show their support, prompting hundreds of emails, picture after picture of lit candles.

Still, my body trembled. I'd done my best to banish dark thoughts, but now profound fear seemed to radiate deep from my core. Seven neo-natal intensive care (NICU) nurses and doctors were lined up, ready to whisk our newborn son away.

It wasn't until Jose entered the delivery room decked out in scrubs, fully energised, that I began to relax. If he could be brave, then I could be too. We were in this together.

Minutes later, I heard Jose rejoice, 'Look, Maggie, look!'

Held above me, in the hands of the doctor, I found our baby. *Pedro*. I reached out my finger and touched his; he grabbed on, and I released a flood of tears.

'He looks good, Maggie,' said the NICU doctor.

That evening, we held onto this strand of hope as Pedro, hours old, was taken for an MRI. I imagined him, a tiny, unknowing bundle beneath the huge magnet.

Within a few days, it was official. Our son's brain was full, complete, perfect.

Eight years later, I still say our Pedro came to Earth on a lightning bolt, jettisoned by all those prayers, led by the shimmer of one hundred candles.

Even Jose, who is not a religious man, calls our son a miracle.

I Had Been Seen
Lisa Birch

I loved looking for signs from God. I had seen them regularly as a child and as a teenager. As a young adult I asked for signs to answer questions like *Am I on the right path? Will I make it through uni? Am I supposed to be a teacher?*

God isn't in the business of fortune-telling, though I wanted him to be. When I was doing my final teaching placement, to absolutely nobody's surprise apart from my own, I was told I wouldn't be passing.

Was I meant to be a teacher? Why would I feel called to this vocation, study for four years, only to be told I wouldn't pass the very last thing I needed to do? None of talking-my-way-around it would change anyone's mind. I was allowed to re-sit my final placement but I would have to wait an entire year. At the time I didn't see this as the privilege it was.

My signs from God had always been tangible. A blooming flower. White cockatoos flying over a car wreck my family walked away from. A well-timed phone call preventing me from making a dangerous mistake. Other people I knew found Bible references in unexpected places, or visions, or had prophetic words spoken over their lives. Where was mine when I needed it most?

The night I found out I had failed my placement I was restless. I didn't want to be alone but I was too ashamed to call anyone and explain what happened. I went for a drive in the rain to get some orange juice, my cure-all during uni years for heartbreak, colds and the flu. I got the OJ but I kept driving through the Adelaide city centre and all the way to Rymill Park before turning the car back in the direction it was supposed to be going –

homeward bound. I came home, drank my juice, and went to sleep. All my life I had told myself, 'Things will be better in the morning,' but this time it wasn't true. I still had to get up and teach my students knowing I wouldn't be rewarded for my effort.

A couple of weeks later I ran into a friend. 'I saw you drive past uni a couple of weeks ago. I was waiting to be picked up…it was so cold…What were you doing?'

'Just driving,' I told her, and then changed the subject. *I saw you. I saw you. I saw you.* Eleven years later and my eyes always well up at this memory. Even in my brokenness and failure I was seen.

That was my sign. It wasn't a signpost or a proof-of-promise like I had regularly sought. I stopped looking for signs and started accepting God in the here and now. The God who witnesses failure, and loves me regardless.

I did re-sit my teaching placement – and passed it. But as for signs – well, I didn't need them anymore. I had been seen.

My Shadow
Ruth C. Hall

I have a Shadow.

It has loomed dark and foreboding in my life, hovering over my shoulder. Sitting so heavily on me, grinding me, pushing me to the ground. For many years it held me captive.

Somehow it came between me and those I love. It stole many things from me. My dear children and then grandchildren. Holding them, knowing I loved them, but why couldn't I feel that love?

Leave me alone, Shadow – you are not my friend!

Church was hard, with this Shadow dogging everything I did. I couldn't feel God. Friendships tested. Family kindnesses stretched. Too hard for people to understand the torment and power that the Shadow had over me. Too easy to judge my failures and weaknesses.

The doctors had a name for it. Severe Treatment-Resistant Depression. They thought it might be tamed with medication. Lots of it. Big doses. It would quieten for a while, but it always came back. They thought maybe shock therapy would scare it away. It didn't.

How does one get rid of a Shadow like this one? It hurt me. Inside. The pain it attacked me with was so real. My heart ached so deeply, so physically. Deep sadness. Hopelessness.

Counselling, prayer ministry – nothing made this Shadow go. It would slink off for a while at times. Then I'd feel I was almost 'normal', that I could achieve things, reach my potential, live a normal life. People would see the real me. Months would go by with only an occasional glimpse of the Shadow peeking around the wall of my soul. I would start to feel again, and I even had times of happiness.

But, just when I thought maybe this time I was free, suddenly, a huge dark foreboding, and I knew it was back. For no reason. Where had it gone? What had I done to bring it back this time?

This dark Shadow tried to take away my faith. It didn't succeed. When I had nothing, I clung to my God. Worship music – my lifeline. It didn't take the Shadow away, just silenced it for a short time.

Suicide attempts…it almost won. In the worst times the Shadow loomed convincingly over me. Twisting my thinking: my loved ones would be much better off without me; the burden of me and my Shadow; there was heaven waiting with no more pain.

But now the years have passed, time has moved on. I have fought a gruelling fight and I have endured. Stayed alive. Once so massive, so much a part of my life, this cruel Shadow has somehow faded.

It has lost its power over me. Now just a reflection of the Shadow it used to be. Still around but not taking over. The Shadow may always be with me. But it is never my friend.

And all that time I thought it was just me and my Shadow. But I see now, it was my God, me and the shadow.

My Protector
Karen Curran

As a child, I counted on my bed sheet for protection. Tucked under on all sides, it held the ghosts at bay. With every inch of its edges sealed between my body and the mattress, I knew nothing – not even a vapour – could get me. I had no doubt there were ghosts. So many people had died over the course of time, there were surely some whose spirits roamed. And I believed there was truth to those Casper cartoons – good ghost, bad ghost. The Ghostly Trio.

But I never imagined I had seen a ghost until Paper Karen came to my house. My kindergarten teacher had students trace each other on sheets of brown paper which we coloured to look like ourselves and then cut out. All the paper students were fastened on the classroom walls until that fateful day when the teacher sent them to our homes and my delighted mother taped mine on my closet door, opposite the foot of my twin bed. At night, with the faint hallway light glowing around the edges of the bedroom door, I could see the dim shape of a person at my closet. Because of limited light and sleepy eyes, I couldn't tell that it was just a picture of me, didn't recognise the smile that greeted me in the mirror every morning or my favourite blue dress. It was just an image girded by the doorframe, impossible to tell if it was going or coming, or even if the door was open or closed. *Who is in my room? Is that a ghost? A person? Are they coming to get me?* I would gasp, then pull the sheet over and under my head and tuck it in, making a seal around my body.

Small children usually call to their parents for help, but heaven forbid that I make a sound and draw attention to myself. Plus, I had already learned my parents might not be there. My sister was at school one day, my dad was at work, and Mother had put me down for a nap. When I called out to ask permission to use the bathroom, there was no answer. I finally crept from my room and wandered through the house but couldn't find Mother. I was alone. My first impulse was to run get under my covers, but I realised I couldn't watch for my mother from the bedroom, so instead stationed myself at the front window. We had a picture window in our living room that came nearly to the floor, in front of which sat a coffee table. I took shelter under the table, and huddled there, peering through the bottom of that window. I made myself as small as possible, hoping that no one could see me, either from inside or outside the house. I cried silently, careful to not alert any intruder or ghost to my whereabouts. I longed for my mother to come back to me. Bereft, abandoned, yet hopeful.

When Mother came home what seemed a lifetime later, she didn't comfort me in an embrace but, instead, chastised me for not taking a nap. I'd been told I had to nap if I wanted to stay up past the usual bedtime to join my sister in watching a television show she was required to watch for school. I cried myself to sleep that night, trying to drown out the faint noise from the TV in the next room.

The discovery that my parents couldn't be counted on shook me. *Who would keep me safe?* In their efforts to assuage my fears (and possibly their guilt), Mother and Daddy pointed me to God, saying he was the only one who was always there, the only one I could completely depend on. They began teaching me the 23rd Psalm. *The Lord is my shepherd.* They said I needed to trust the God to whom we prayed at meals and at bedtime. And I did. I took their words as truth and was fervent in my prayers, imagining my

My Protector

mouth speaking directly into God's ear. I believed he was listening, though invisible. At night when I saw the figure at my closet door, I wrapped myself in my bedsheet cocoon to block everything else out of sight, and would lie there tucked in for hours, in what I felt were God's arms, while whispering parts of the Psalm over and over.

The Lord is my shepherd; I shall not want. Yea, though I walk through the valley of the shadow of death, I will fear no evil; for thou art with me.

I clung to those words, safe in my sheet.

One night, I told myself there was nothing to fear beyond my covering; one peek would prove it. But a frightened mind can do some conjuring. I turned my head, loosed the sheet, and peered out. There beside my bed was a white figure. It was wearing a ten-gallon hat and holding a six-shooter in one hand, a knife in the other, and even without his bushy moustache being red, I recognised the ghost of Yosemite Sam. Tall as my father and so real, I could have reached out and touched him. He stared down at me, murder gleaming in his eyes.

No. It couldn't be. Why would he come for me? I wasn't his despised Bugs Bunny, just a kid who liked cartoons. I stifled a scream while yanking the bed sheet back in place.

Help, God! The Lord is my shepherd, I shall not want. The Lord is my shepherd.

I said it over and over, eventually falling asleep. Next thing I knew, it was morning. Yosemite Sam was gone, the picture I now recognised as myself was smiling sweetly from the closet door, and I felt perfectly calm. My prayers had worked. My Good Shepherd had proven he would keep me safely through the night.

It's funny that, sixty-some years later, the cat who shares the bed with my husband and me also goes undercover when he's frightened. I'm glad the Good Shepherd can be counted on to care for us all.

Just in Time
Colleen Russell

I waited at the hospital window, watched as you hurried up the path. I smiled at the sun shining on your hair, smiled at the smile on your face, exactly as I first saw you on that first lovely day, as you came to visit someone else here.

Hurry, hurry – late again.

But you found me as well. And I found you, found your understanding and your love – just in time.

That day you came into my life and changed my loneliness. You took away my deepest doubts, chased away my dread and fears and set me on the path I was seeking.

You showed me the way.

So now I know where I'm going and the reason I've been put on this earth. I don't have to wonder anymore, because you've found me and I have found you.

And now you're here.

'I'm ready to cash in me chips,' Gramps used to say as he grew older, 'and I've crossed all me bridges.' But he wasn't one for giving up and persisted well into his nineties.

My bridges were broken apart and all my rivers flowed on turbulent courses downhill on their way to nowhere, and my thoughts seemed to flow along with them.

I felt that my time was running out. I was ready to give up, ready to 'cash in me chips'.

But when queried, Gramps would also have advised, 'Just get on with it, luv. Have yourself a natter with God. He's there, you know, listening, he's always listening.'

Sounds simple enough. But sometimes in my darkest hours, when the demons cowered in the corners of my mind, the simplest things became the most difficult to achieve.

Before you came, that is, when my days were long and my nights even longer.

I couldn't remember the prayers from my childhood; wasn't sure how to go about 'nattering' to The Man. So I mumbled a few requests, apologising for my ignorance and clumsy appeals.

'I'm sorry to bother you, God, but pleasehelpme, pleasehelpme, pleasehelpme!'

Then one sunny morning I stood at the hospital window, watching as you hurried up the path. And you smiled and you waved, and I knew – you'd found me.

'I'm sorry, I'm late,' you said breathlessly.

'No, no, as long as you are here – and you're just in time.'

Immanuel: Not Just a Christmas Story
Claire Bell

'You're going to have to call an ambulance.' Until that moment, I had been hoping my back pain would recede and we could get on with the day's plan to visit nearby waterfalls.

My husband did so, and soon I was breathing through a 'green whistle' (anaesthetic) and transported to a hospital in rural New South Wales.

We were four days into an interstate camping trip, the first of many intended in our new retirement. With heavy rains forecast, we had decided to stow the tent in favour of a motel in Armidale. On our first morning, my back seized in the shower when, ironically, I was doing my daily back stretches. Within minutes I could not move any muscle without agony.

I was terrified of moving, and of not being able to move. We were strangers here, far from our Adelaide home and our Sydney relatives. It was nearing Christmas, in a quiet phase of the Covid-19 pandemic, and with all the usual pre-Christmas busyness and holiday closures that make life more complicated than usual.

The paramedics and the hospital staff were sympathetic, and the advice was simple: move. Painkillers and anti-inflammatory drugs served that one purpose.

So that was my focus for the next six weeks, from the first day when I shuffled from the hospital to the motel (2.6km in one hour and forty minutes), to the short car hops with walk breaks until we finally reached Sydney, and all the restlessness of changing positions on chairs and beds until the herniated disc healed.

On that first day, standing with my back to the bedroom mirror in the motel, frozen with pain and fear, I recognised Immanuel in my circumstances. The muscle spasms had happened in Armidale, a town with a hospital and an ambulance service, not in the Warrumbungles where we had camped the previous days. We were staying in a motel, not in a tent. The motel we chose was in walking distance of town, not one of the lovely accommodations further out.

In the midst of adversity, I knew I was being cared for, that God was present and leading me through this narrow, dark chasm. The way was challenging and I was emotionally fragile. My husband was a wonderful support, but God was with me on the inside where no one else could reach, deeper than my fear, more constant than my pain.

God was with me.

Pinball
Tsung Chung

Life is not meant to be this precarious.

This random, this unpredictable. We could be going along our merry way when – WHAM! – we are suddenly flat on our back, wondering what just happened. Then the pain starts to register, and the unstable surroundings continue to rock us.

Still, Bouncy Castles have always been popular. At the Community Centre's Fun Day, the long line of children willing to risk life and limb was a testament to the attractiveness of danger. My job as The Attendant of The Bouncy Castle was to keep them safe, monitoring their chaotic misadventures within that fifteen square metres of Enclosed Peril.

The corners were a constant threat as combatants congregating there caused the structure to tilt alarmingly. Inevitably, the others would gleefully join them, and the castle would groan sadly, caught in the battle between concentrated gravity and compressed air.

Spread out, I implored.

No pushing, I barked.

Stop having so much fun, I left unsaid.

Even the escape to safety was fraught with hazard. Kids tumbled down the exit ramp like pinballs in a machine, bumping into every inflatable step. Giddy with excitement and armed with a supreme sense of indestructibility, they bolted to the back of the line awaiting another 120 seconds of mayhem.

One of the pinballs, however, veered off. He made a beeline to Mum and tearfully nestled into her arms, coming out worse for wear from an accident in the Danger Zone. I approached Mum, explaining the likely collision of heads. Her smile told me it was not too serious.

Still, my heart sank a little. Failure in carrying out proper duty of care as The Attendant of The Bouncy Castle was not something to be taken lightly.

Resolutely, I continued to pace the outer boundary, scouring with renewed earnestness for the slightest stirrings of jeopardy. Fifteen minutes passed without further incident when I caught sight of the wayward pinball in full flight – jumping, bouncing, laughing as if his recent head trauma had never happened.

Mum wasn't too far away, quietly observing. I slid across to her, not taking my eye off the action, expressing my surprise in seeing him back inside.

'He just needed to cry it out,' I heard Mum say beside me.

'Don't we all?' I thought.

It took me a moment to realise that I was wrong – I hadn't thought it, I had blurted it out. Where did that come from? I was there to man the Inflatable Menace, not to share my secret coping methods. Once verbalised, however, it could not be taken back. I slowly turned to face Mum, expecting an awkward look and bracing myself for an uncomfortable silence.

Instead, a sheepish smile spread across Mum's face as she confessed, 'I do it myself sometimes.'

Both my worried look and her embarrassed smile transformed into understanding nods. No further words were needed, and we quietly turned our attention back to the castle.

In that moment, life somehow felt a little safer.

Twenty
Robert Riggs

About two years ago, I came clean to my wife of twenty-something years about a number of extramarital affairs I'd had over a seven-year stretch.

I'll just let that sit there for a few seconds.

I can hear your voice in my head and I don't even know you.

'What is wrong with you?'

'Why on earth did you do that?'

'Don't you have any self-control?'

It gets worse.

I was raised in the church, taught godly values and have even been baptised. I knew then what marriage meant to God and man, and I agreed with those values. In fact, my whole life I've had a personal relationship with Jesus Christ.

And I still committed adultery.

More than once.

With different women.

After thirteen years of marriage.

I had somehow managed to convince myself that this was okay, that this double life could go on undetected and that I – no, we – would be fine.

I was so wrong.

For all the time I lived with those secrets, my life was in turmoil and my marriage was becoming diseased – by my own hand. Trying to conceal not only my sin but also my actions, which were in direct contrast to my values, was a compounding and traumatising experience.

I had even prayed amongst all this sin for help living with it. To help me forget it, to help me move forward with my life as if nothing had ever happened. More misguided self-belief. I would journal my daily struggles without actually addressing the problem. I would write about why my wife didn't understand me and question why this life was so difficult. I was searching for someone to blame without looking in the mirror, longing for answers I already had.

Then early one morning, as I left a woman in a hotel room in the city… a spiritual awakening…

'This is not who you are.' Simple and unwavering.

'No.' I negotiated with the persistent thought. I knew where this was going.

'You can make this right,' the thought continued.

'No, I can't…and she'll leave.'

'But that's the price of your actions, isn't it?'

'Well…yes…of course…but…'

'Do you believe this is who you are – whom I formed – whom I saw?'

The thought crushed me as I already knew the answer. I'd become everything I never ever wanted to be – a full and complete copy of my father, minus the domestic violence, but who knows how long that would have lasted.

I was drunk and overcome with emotion.

'I *still* believe in you.'

I sobbed like a lost little boy in a crowd of people. *I don't deserve this unconditional acceptance, not after everything I've done.* A drunken taxi ride home from the city broke me. I guess grace knows no boundaries.

Twenty

I got out of that taxi and left my old life behind.

It took me two days and some very wise counsel before I found the courage to tell my wife everything.

It was about 10pm on a Monday night. I sat opposite my wife, on the couch, uncomfortable.

'I have something to tell you,' I said.

I could feel the lump in the back of my throat. I could tell that this was really, really going to hurt.

The gaps between my sentences seemed to go on for hours.

I looked everywhere except at her and felt my breath weighing me down like an anchor.

I was so scared, so lost.

'I have to…to tell you something,' I repeated.

Her face dropped. She could see how uncharacteristic this moment was, that bad news was imminent. I could see her mind ticking over. It was like she knew what I was going to say but didn't want to hear me say it. Going back through her memories trying to identify the signs she'd already seen but refused to believe – until right now.

'Stop!' she let out. Tears were streaming down her face.

My masculine exterior became mush as her voice restrained me from bringing my sin into the light. It broke my heart to be caught in the middle of her devastation while also being responsible for it.

'I'm so sorry…' I trailed off, trying not to cry.

More of the longest silence ever.

Like a queue in a department store sale, those moments I'd spent with other women were there in the room with us, lined up, waiting to collect their dues. I didn't have a leg to stand on. I could ask nothing of her. Whatever her choice was going to be, I was going to support her. That was my new mandate, and I was obliged.

I tried to settle my mind, my breathing still heavy. I never, ever saw this in our future.

I was stalling. I needed to own my decisions, as any real man would.

'I have...lost my way,' I started again.

I tried as hard as I could to ease into the facts. I told her about each and every mistake as she probed for more detailed information. I searched my memories so I could share this hidden life with her, though it repulsed me to do so.

In little over an hour, I had torn her beating heart out of her chest and trampled all over it.

'Go,' she said at last, broken, distraught and confused.

I walked out of the house expecting no less and got into my car as the heavens opened. I made a decision right there to call my mother-in-law, and while not sharing any detail, I asked if she could call her daughter immediately. I *will* support her – my new mandate.

I put the car into reverse and started to back out of the driveway when there was a knock on the passenger side window.

My wife.

'What are you doing out here, hun...it's raining,' I said with a softness I hadn't felt in a long time. She opened the door and got into the car, a wet mess.

We sat in silence again.

Twenty

'Thank you for telling me the truth,' she finally said.

'You don't owe me thanks,' I replied.

We continued in silence, watching the windows steam up and the rain fall.

It was another incredibly spiritual moment, and for the first time in a long time, I prayed in the company of my wife.

'God – I have wronged you and my wife, and I'm sorry.'

My wife didn't say anything else to me after that, but she did draw a broken heart in the steam on the glass before she got out of my car.

I was king in the court of the unworthy.

I wanted to stay with her, I wanted to help her but I knew it wasn't my call to make. It was her call, and I was going to support her no matter what. It felt strange – an unburdened feeling mixed with pain, humility, sorrow, peace and love. I had confessed my sin and was ready to pay the price in full.

Enter the immeasurable extension of grace, complete only in the undeserving.

Over the next two years I remained steadfast in my new mandate. We rebuilt our marriage, as I recovered my life and what it means to be a man. I have drawn closer to my wife, sharing my work, my phone and my laptop. I've been completely open, avoiding weakness and temptation, encouraged by her love and support. With both hands I have held tightly to the grace my wife and my God have extended to me.

Just like the thorn in Paul's side, the constant awareness that I did not deserve a second chance inspires me every day to be better, to try harder. And for that I am truly thankful.

An Unseen Guide
Craig Chapman

Months earlier, we'd dubbed it 'J-day' in anticipation of the battle to reach the summit of Mt Jagungal, deep in the Kosciuszko National Park wilderness. Now, early on day four of our epic six day hike, we were experiencing brutal confirmation of our expectations.

We'd prepared well, tailoring some of our training specifically for this part of the adventure. Now the doubts were swirling in my mind, and, as evidenced by the uncharacteristic lack of chatter behind me, in the minds of my hiking buddies. I could imagine what they were thinking. *Does our leader know what he's doing? Is this a bad idea?*

The first few hours had gone well enough. The heavy overnight snowfall had given way to clear sky. Spirits were high and there were numerous memorable photo opportunities. Now, progress had slowed to a crawl as we struggled through dense scrub, saturated from the waist down. The prospect of having wet boots for the rest of the day, possibly longer, wasn't improving the team's collective morale.

The track was, at best, poorly defined. Parting the chest-high, barely-penetrable bush with my hands resulted in nothing more than occasional fleeting glimpses four or five metres ahead. Touch was my most valuable sense as I navigated by feeling the groove of the track with my feet. However, we were now battling the clock as well as the terrain. *Could we reach this summit before making the long journey to our next campsite?*

An Unseen Guide

I silently consulted God in prayer. As always, we'd begun the day asking him to guide us. Hope rose in me as I remembered the unlikely encounter with a park ranger the day before. If either party had been even slightly delayed, the conversation at a remote track intersection would never have happened. The advice he offered had caused me to wonder if he might have been an angel. He'd looked human enough. *So did the angels in the Bible*, I thought, recalling the story of Abraham entertaining guests, oblivious to their heavenly identity. Eyeing our heavy packs, the ranger had convinced us that what appeared to be a short cut on the map was not worth the risk. *Thanks, Lord. Please speak to us again.*

With great relief, we finally exited the thick scrub. I scanned the snowy trail ahead, noticing the unmistakable footprints of a wombat heading up the mountain. The snow had only fallen a few hours ago. Had God sent a wombat to lead us to the summit?

We followed the wombat's tracks for nearly an hour. Only on the final rocky scramble a few metres below the top had our four-legged guide apparently wandered into the wilderness.

The elation of summiting was short-lived. After a speedy descent, we gulped down some lunch and strapped on our packs to trek the remaining fourteen kilometres to our campsite, arriving after dark. By then, the realisation had sunk in. God isn't limited to using humans or even angels to guide us.

The Gift
Juni Desireé Hoel

I moved from the suburbs of Melbourne to a small country beach town in Queensland where no-one knew me. There were no expectations of what I should be like, and I was keen to make friends and encourage people instead of sitting alone too timid to speak.

I geared myself up to attend a Pilates class and not just keep to myself but introduce myself and cheer people on. It all went wrong. Every time I tried to talk to someone, they brushed me off. At the end of the class, I tried again. I said hello and introduced myself to the lady next to me. She looked at me like I was an interruption. She said an abrupt hello then started talking to the people behind us. I stood there wondering if they might include me in the conversation. The lady turned to me and said with no hint of a smile, 'Okay, well it was nice meeting you,' and turned back to the others. I stood there like a fool.

I left demoralised.

Since I knew what it was like to feel left out and rejected, I never wanted anyone else to feel this way. I wanted to do my part and give people a smile, initiate conversation, and listen to them to show them they are valued and accepted. But my fear of rejection was still there. It took so much effort to work up the courage to approach people.

I drove to the beach to be alone and cry. I sat on a bench at a picnic table, facing the ocean. I was confused. I didn't want to keep putting in the effort. The rejection hurt too much. I wanted to crawl back into my shell. But maybe I should keep showing up even

The Gift

though it was scary because maybe someone out there needed to know they're accepted.

'Do I keep putting myself out there?' I asked God.

A boy and his mum wandered past. The boy stopped and sat on the bench opposite me on the other side of the table. His mum continued walking towards the water. When she realised he wasn't with her, she turned around.

'Come on,' she called. 'Let's go down to the water.'

The boy didn't acknowledge her. Instead, he brushed sand off the table. He never looked at me. Not even when I said, 'Hello,' and smiled at him.

His mum kept coaxing him to go see the water. He kept brushing sand off the table. Then he stood up, picked up a coconut seed from the sand and put it on the table in front of me.

'Is that a gift?' his mum said. 'Good boy. Come on.'

The boy skipped back to his mum. She put her arm around him as they walked to the water. And there I was, left with this gift of acceptance from a boy putting himself out there.

My First Sprout of Faith
Janice D. Green

'Is everyone ready to go?' Dad called out on Sunday morning. All seven of us would soon pile into the car and ride to town for church.

With my dress on and my hair combed, I looked for my shoes. I scrambled up the stairs of our farmhouse for one more look under my bed. I dashed downstairs and checked every room again wondering where I might have kicked them off. Then I remembered kicking them off in the field on Saturday.

I didn't want to miss church, but I couldn't go barefoot either. I loved my church, especially my Sunday School class. 'Please wait for me,' I pleaded with Dad as I dashed off to the field behind the barn where we hoed the green beans and caught the bugs we found on the leaves the day before.

I ran up one row and down another searching for my shoes. I had to find them there. The only thing my slip-on shoes were good for in the field was for catching dirt that rubbed against my toes and feet. I'd kicked them off and gone barefoot.

Our family struggled in 1955. We moved to my father's family farm while Dad changed careers. He needed more college classes to complete his teacher certification. No extra pair of shoes fitted in the budget for any of us.

Like a love-starved child, I looked forward to standing with Rev Hill after church as he shook everyone's hand. He always made me feel special. I just had to find my shoes!

Breathless, I ran up and down each long row one more time. Nothing.

My First Sprout of Faith

Fighting tears, I thought about my Sunday school class, when an idea flashed through my mind. God is supposed to answer our prayers. Maybe, just maybe, he would hear my prayer and help me find my shoes.

With my hands folded together and my eyes closed, my prayer went like this, 'God, if you are really there, and if you really do answer prayers, would you please help me find my shoes?' I remember that prayer like it was yesterday – my first real step of faith.

I opened my eyes, turned around, and started to go back down the row of beans, but I didn't have to take another step before I saw them. 'Thank you, God!' There on the ground lay my precious dusty orangey-yellow shoes in plain sight. I quickly slid my feet into them and ran toward the house.

Yes! The car was still in the driveway. They waited!

Did I run too fast to see my shoes before I prayed? Did an angel move them to that spot behind me so I could see them better? I'll never know the answer to those questions. But I knew from that moment on that God does answer prayers, even the desperate prayer of a little girl who can't find her shoes.

Who Would You Choose?
Jenine Altmann

The engine shuddered to a halt as the exhaust belched its last few fumes for the day. I abandoned the mower to sit and lean against the weathered veranda post. Surveying the newly cut grass gave me a sense of achievement and satisfaction.

Sunset was beginning to etch its way across the sky. Watching, my thoughts turned to God.

'Just ask,' popped into my mind like an unwanted intruder.

Hesitation gripped me.

'What if the answer is no?' Despite my reservation I quietly started, 'Father, I believe that you can do all things, please…heal me.'

In the hush I expectantly waited.

'If I took your disease and gave it to someone else,' the serene voice asked, 'who would you choose?'

This question took me by surprise. My bone problem, incurable and with rare side effects, would not be a happy present for anybody.

Still, I was reasonably sure I could come up with a solution.

I thought it best to cross people off a list – easier to eliminate than build a list of possibilities. My immediate and extended family were easily crossed off my mental list. Friends, acquaintances and church family were the next major players eliminated. Now I was down to people who annoyed me and those I felt needed to learn a lesson. My smug attitude was bothering me, so I crossed them off the list as well.

Surely I needed to think on a broader spectrum. It would be safer for me to choose someone I had never met.

Who Would You Choose?

There were people who have been incarcerated. The homeless and the disadvantaged also crossed my mind. Would it make a huge difference to them? Or maybe I should think about those who live the 'high life' – those who seem to have more than they need. Perhaps it would help them to understand that life can be difficult.

Shame washed over me as I realised how low my attitude had sunk. Who was I to judge the people I don't know? How would I know the effects on their mental, emotional or spiritual wellbeing? Everybody has their burden, whether or not it is on display for others to see. God cares for all people in all circumstances, including me.

The sun was slipping below the horizon and gentle dusk was claiming the sky.

'I can't think of anyone,' I whispered to God.

'I never expected you would,' came the gentle reply. I realised the question had not been an offer but a catalyst. I am sure God smiled along with me as I left the veranda to take a nice hot shower.

That evening the question I had been asking changed. It turned from 'Why me?' to 'Why not me?' I am a cracked pot, but I have good company. Paul, who had 'a thorn in the flesh', also received a 'No' when he asked for healing. Even so, God gives us the mercy we need to live.

Tears for a Baby
Jo Wanmer

A tear dropped. Onto the baby's cheek. I kissed it away, dropping more tears on Bea's tiny face. Tissues – they must be somewhere in this hospital room, but I resorted to paper towel as the nurses always did.

I was alone in the room with two baby girls. One was just a day old; the other, the one I cuddled, was three weeks older, but no bigger. As my daughter's driver, I had come to visit her friend, a young girl who had just delivered her second baby. Another teenage mother was also visiting, bringing baby Bea. The three young women went outside to smoke and chat leaving me to watch the babies.

As I cuddled baby Bea, my heart broke. Her mother was single and lived on the edge of the drug world. Her father was doubtful. Why should any baby have to overcome such odds? At three weeks she was under two and a half kilos. What could I do for this little waif? As kidnapping wasn't an option, I started to pray.

That's when the tears fell, baptising her with the Father's love. What could he do? I had no idea but I stormed heaven on her behalf.

Through my daughter, I followed her development from afar. She had a brother, Bob, who was just twenty months older.

When Bea was ten months, her mother left her and Bob at their father's house. On Christmas Eve at 8pm. Without notice. He was drunk, so, for their safety, he put them in a bedroom until the morning. The mother left no bottles. No supplies. No pram.

Somehow the father coped and Bea survived. When my daughter reported this turn of events, I nearly rang the authorities, but my knowledge was second hand and my girl promised to watch out for them.

'He's doing okay with them, Mum. If Bea wants a hug she crawls up on his knee.'

Photos showed sad eyes, skinny body and stringy hair. My arms longed to hold this precious life, still so tiny. More tearful prayers.

My daughter continued to visit, to care for them, to take them to the mall to have their photos taken. The mother? She never returned.

One night, they came for dinner. We sat outside on the veranda. The children were nervous, hiding behind their equally nervous daddy. The second time they came, they warmed to me a little. On the third visit my daughter told us she was engaged to their father and was moving in with him to care for the children. I was flabbergasted, shocked and devastated until I sought the Lord.

He reminded me that I had prayed. He was answering.

And so, not long after she turned two, in a garden wedding, Bea became my granddaughter. And years later, she presented me with my first great-grandchildren. God answered me beyond what I could ask, think, or even imagine. He truly is amazing.

Set Free from Darkness
Ket Pang

About eight years ago, I fell into a dark abyss. My relationship with my family had deteriorated to a point that I could never have imagined. I was surrounded by negativity, feeling frightened and insecure. Deep down, I was miserable. I suffered depression and was having suicidal thoughts. I hid this from everyone by covering it with anger.

A few years on, my wife started going to church. I was an atheist and refused to go to any church. Every Sunday, I sat in the car and waited for her. On one very hot day, instead of waiting outside the church, I decided to go inside because of the air conditioning. I didn't worship but just sat there. The next week, I went inside the church again, and again the following week, and so on. Eventually, I found myself enjoying the sermons.

One night, darkness and sadness overwhelmed me. I couldn't bear it anymore. I stormed out of the house. I ran for miles, crying in despair, until I got up to a small hill in complete darkness. I looked up the stars in the sky. I was crying hysterically and said, 'God, if you're listening, if you're there, I really, really need your help, please fix me, please take me away, I don't want to be here anymore…' As I turned around, I saw city lights in front of me, and within a minute, I felt a strong and warm sensation going through my chest, followed by an overwhelming flood of joy. All of a sudden, I was extremely happy, and moved from crying in despair to crying for joy. It all happened so quickly, just like flipping on a light switch. I knew that I wasn't on any medication, and at that moment, all I wanted to do was to rush home as I couldn't wait to tell my wife and kids how much I loved them. It felt as if I had not seen them for years, as if I had been locked away in darkness all that time.

Since that night, I have had a sense of contentment that I had not known before. I know that I have been healed. The almighty God healed me. The darkness is gone and has not returned. Since that night, I have hardly missed a Sunday church service. Church is like a hospital for my soul. It is also a battery charging station for my spiritual well-being.

In 2018 I accepted Christ at an event organised by the church. God has delivered me out of darkness, healed me and turned me into a new person and I know he is able to do much more than I can imagine. I have received a new peace and joy from above that the world can't give to me. My relationship with my family has turned around in a way I wouldn't have thought possible. Love has entered and warmed our home.

Incident at Peats Ridge
Jonathan Mowen

I was twenty-two and dreaming of heaven on earth. I hoped I would find it at Peats Ridge Music Festival. It was, after all, one of the 'world's leading sustainability events' and if a sustainable job or relationship somehow materialised from me attending, I could once and for all confirm that heaven's miracles were accessible in the present age.

I woke early on the last day of the festival, New Year's Day 2010. I drove up the S-bends that snaked their way up the escarpment and looked out at the lush green valley below. Rows of tents, hundreds of eucalypts, a glimpse of golden sun…

I dedicated the new year to God, considered my plans and asked for God's blessing.

I sang a verse or two of 'Battle Hymn of the Republic', then heard a car throttling hard, the sound seeming to come from the valley below. I couldn't believe this car was driving so fast, especially if it was coming up the S-bends. Then I heard no car.

It was odd how quickly the car had stopped and I got a feeling something was wrong. I considered the newspaper headlines the next day: 'Fatal Accident at Music Festival'. This was enough to inspire me to start back down the road.

Soon, I saw a 4WD flipped and steaming. I got out of my car and dialled 000. A bedraggled man from the car approached and said 'Don't worry about that'.

In a panic, I said, 'Sure,' and hung up.

He said, 'Can you give me a lift?'

'Of course.'

He got in, said his name.
I said, 'I'm Jon.'
He said 'Are you Christian?'
I said, 'Yep.
He said, 'Were you praying?'
'Yep.'
He said, 'If you weren't praying, I think I would be dead right now. I'm a dickhead, but I believe in God.'

This guy proceeded to tell me he had been married recently, had had a drunken argument with his wife over New Year's Eve, got into the car in a rage, flipped it and was being taken by me to his father-in-law's for whom he was planning to conduct a most unenviable apology.

*I'm a dickhead, but I believe in God...*CS Lewis couldn't have said it better.

I dropped old mate off a little way down the M1 between Newcastle and Sydney and started my new year very grateful for my little glimpse of heaven.

I Dined in Style
Helena Stretton

When the doorbell rang, there I found a Coles delivery man with three large bags of groceries – one of dairy goods, one of packets and tins, and a third with fresh foods! Plus two coveted toilet rolls!

'I didn't order these!' I said.

'Lucky you!' he replied, smiling.

A former student of mine from forty years ago, now living in Perth (I'm in Adelaide) had recalled that I would now be in the vulnerable age range for catching the Covid-19 virus (I'm 81), and probably living alone (I am), so shouldn't be going into supermarkets. So she ordered the surprise grocery gift!

As a result, that night I dined in style at the hotel 'Strathmore' (the name of my house), commencing with a sparkling drink, then roast chicken, chips and roast veggies, followed by blueberry twist yoghurt, fresh rockmelon and grapes, and concluding with a latte coffee and chocolates!

I felt like a queen! What thoughtfulness! What generosity!

When I later thanked her profusely, she said, 'God nudged me.' So with deep gratitude I praised them both!

Fishing for Faith
R.J. Rodda

'I hope we get a fish this time, Mummy,' said my five year old son Samuel, his blue eyes serious. We were camping on an isolated hill in a national park and were about to head down to the river.

'Me too,' I said, trying to keep my voice upbeat. Every time my boys had gone fishing the result had been the same: no fish. They would march off enthusiastically and return disappointed. My husband frequently declared fishing was a waste of time but the boys were so keen, it was hard to say no.

'Why don't we pray God helps you catch a fish?' I said.

Samuel nodded and dashed out a prayer before running down to the water's edge. James, his older brother, was already casting his fishing line under the supervision of my husband. Then Samuel's fishing rod was set up too.

Soon seven year old James' line got snagged. He tried to reel it in but it flicked back and the bright red three-pronged lure caught in his chin. He tried to pull it out himself, but only embedded it further into his flesh. My husband jiggled it, as James tried not to cry, but it was wedged so deeply that the prongs were not visible.

So we abandoned everything and scrambled into the car, driving to the nearest hospital. James was calm, seeming almost to enjoy the distinction of having a lure in his chin and looking forward to telling all the kids at school about it.

Once at the hospital, the staff took over, numbing James' chin before pulling out the lure. Meanwhile, I revelled in the small luxuries available: air-conditioning, a flush toilet and liquid soap.

When James emerged, his wound was glued and he was clutching a specimen jar containing the extracted lure.

We drove back to camp. Once there, the boys remembered the fishing lines left in the lake. They ran down excitedly to check, dragging my husband with them. They were always hopeful despite all experience to the contrary.

My husband began to reel in Samuel's line and there was a tug at the other end. There was a fish on it! A real fish that flapped around in the water. The boys were ecstatic and shouted for joy. Samuel had caught his first fish, his hope had been justified and his prayer had been answered.

Isn't it time you told your story?

This year, 52 people have had their stories published, and nine of them have been recognised as category winners. Do you have a story of faith and testimony? Will 2022 be the year you tell your story?

For the possibility of being published or winning a prize, please send us your true stories in one of these three categories:

Short Stories of Life
(up to 500 words)

Young Stories of Life
(500 – 1000 words for writers aged 17 and under)

Open Stories of Life
(1000 – 1500 words)

Submission details, rules and writing resources can be found on our website:

https://storiesoflife.net

Have you written a book?
Not sure how to get it published?
Worried it will cost a fortune?

Not a problem.

Helping writers to become authors

info@immortalise.com.au
www.immortalise.com.au

www.ingramcontent.com/pod-product-compliance
Lightning Source LLC
Chambersburg PA
CBHW072001290426
44109CB00018B/2098